HOW TO FIND AND LAND YOUR FIRST FULL-TIME JOB

HOW TO FIND AND LAND YOUR FIRST FULL-TIME JOB

Leonard Corwen

ARCO PUBLISHING, INC.
NEW YORK

Published by Arco Publishing, Inc.
215 Park Avenue South, New York, N.Y. 10003

Library of Congress Cataloging in Publication Data

Corwen, Leonard.
  How to find and land your first full-time job.

  Bibliography: p.
  Includes index.
  1. Job hunting. I. Title.
HF5382.7.C67   650.1′4   82-6742
ISBN 0-668-05458-1 (Reference Text) AACR2
ISBN 0-668-05463-8 (Paper Edition)

Printed in the United States of America

FOR BERNICE AND CAROL

Contents

Foreword

You are the proud owner of a diploma, degree or certificate attesting to the fact that you are now qualified to offer the world the benefits of your expertise and considerable talents, and you are eagerly, or perhaps reluctantly, about to enter the workaday nine to five world.

Poised on the brink, ready to join the ranks of American wage earners, you will probably feel the same disorientation that almost every first-time job-hunter experiences. Like a sailor at sea you know there is a landfall out there somewhere, but in which direction do you steer? You have completed your training and you are ready and eager to exchange your time and energy for hard cash. You're all dressed up with no place to go.

If this sounds like a harsh appraisal of the conditions facing the new job-hunter, it is, but it is also unfortunately, pretty accurate. It is not intended to discourage you or make you wish you were back in the security of the academic womb. There is a job out there for you. What you need is some professional guidance to help you avoid the pitfalls facing the disorganized and undisciplined job-hunter.

That is what this book is all about. The fact that you are reading it shows that you are seriously concerned about your future. It is designed to provide you, the inexperienced job-seeker, with a step-by-step program with which to find a job.

Upon entering the job market for the first time, there are many choices to be made. Deciding what you want to do is only the first. Where do you want to do it? Are you interested in making a career with a company that manufactures consumer products? What kind? Or do you prefer heavy industry? Do you want to get involved with a firm that sells services, such as advertising, insurance or banking? Do you lean to educational or nonprofit activities? Would you be better off starting with a small firm or a large one? A discussion of the pros and cons of each may help you decide.

Making the best use of your available time is one of the most important problems that you will face. Each week without a job is a week without a paycheck. Time passes quickly enough during normal activities, but when you are in pursuit of the means of earning your living, it rushes by at the speed of a jet stream.

The chapter on effective time management will show you how to use the limited time you have and thereby help you get a job quickly.

How do companies hire? Where do they turn for help in finding new employees? There are many sources for jobs available to the job-hunter. Many are obvious, some less so, and a few almost never used. The largest number of jobs never come to the attention of the general public. These constitute the so-called hidden job market. Knowing where this is and how to reach it puts you several steps ahead of the competition.

Looking for a job can be a lonely undertaking. However, there is plenty of help available if you know where to go. This book tells about the firms, organizations, and individuals whose expertise is available. Many are free, some cost money. Where to find them, how to use them and those to avoid is discussed in the chapter on outside help.

The ticket of admission to almost every interview in today's busy business world is your résumé. How to write one that is informative where you have little or no work experience is the subject of the chapter on the preparation and use of résumés. Special forms are included to help to prepare a résumé that will get you interviews. Samples of successful résumés are included for your guidance.

Very few interviews are granted to the walk-in applicant. All job hunting starts with correspondence of one kind or another. You need to know how to write proper letters of every type: application letters, résumé cover letters, letters seeking information and miscellaneous letters for all occasions. In addition to a description of each of the kinds of letters you will need, examples of actual letters in each category are included for your use.

The face-to-face arena of the interview is where many a true test comes. It is also the place where many qualified and talented people self-destruct. Handling yourself effectively at an interview is a learned skill.

The chapter on interviews will offer some tips on what employers want to see and hear. It will show you how to convince an employer that, although you do not have much experience, are not the holder of three professional degrees and are somewhat less than a genius, not hiring you would be a mistake.

To help you plan your long-range goals, there is a discussion of the general outlook for jobs in the next decade, together with projections for business and industry in certain occupations.

Lastly, there is a directory of sources of information about your chosen occupation.

1
Getting Ready

Job hunting is a full-time occupation. You will probably find it more difficult and demanding than any paid job you eventually get. Unless you have the kind of luck that strikes sweepstakes winners, or have a parent who owns a large business and wants you on the staff, you are going to be the victim of culture shock, rejection shock and plain old human nastiness.

That's the bad news. The good news is that this book will guide you through an easy-to-follow job-finding campaign based on making the most of your education, abilities, and available resources.

Top to Bottom

The biggest obstacle you will have to overcome is the overnight tumble from the heady status of a college or high school senior to the very bottom of the totem pole. It's a long way down in a very short time. Most people make the adjustment with little or no emotional shock. The few who get upset when they are treated less than royally will probably have a tougher time coping with the bureaucratic, cavalier and often discourteous treatment that the job-hunter receives at a time when he or she is most vulnerable. One of the first things you must do is prepare yourself psychologically and try to remember not to take rejection as a personal insult or as part of a conspiracy to keep you unemployed. The key is not to allow it to upset you.

Take the attitude that any company or individual that does not avail themselves of your services, or that treats you in an unprofessional or shabby manner, isn't worthy of you. Keep a high level of self-confidence in your worth and abilities.

Time Is of the Essence

There are many books, pamphlets and articles on the best way to use your time. There are also seminars on the subject. A new branch of consulting has sprung up to deal with time management, and hardly a day goes by when there is not a meeting, symposium, seminar or course dealing with the subject somewhere in the country.

Obviously, the amount of time spent on a project will have a direct bearing on its completion date. But there is a lot more to it than that. It is not only how much time you spend on your job-hunting activities, it's how you use the time that counts most.

Since your objective is to get on somebody's payroll as soon as possible, you should work at it just as you would a "regular" job, spending seven or eight hours a day, five days a week actively conducting your search. Remember, every hour wasted and not used wisely can cost you hard cash. Specific ways to make time work for you are covered in Chapter 2.

What Do You Want to Do?

In determining what you want to do, you have to decide which world you are talking about—your fantasy world or the real world. The fantasy world is a wonderful place where you are a famous novelist, sportscaster, television commentator, race-car driver, astronaut or corporate executive, beloved by all, respected by your peers and rich beyond your wildest dreams.

The real world is the point where you start to make that dream come true. But you have to be prepared to do the hard, boring groundwork first.

It's okay to be a window-shopper when you are buying clothes or appliances. But if you use the same technique in looking for a job, you will be wasting most of your time.

Some people come out of school knowing exactly what kind of work they want to do. They have been trained for a specific profession such as law, medicine, engineering, accounting or marketing. If you are one of them, you can skip this section. However, if you are among the vast number of people coming out of high school with a general diploma, or college with a liberal arts degree, you probably have not completely made up your mind. Having an open mind has a lot of advantages. It allows you to consider all the options that are open to you and be flexible in your choices. You should, at this point, have at least some general ideas about what you want to do.

There is no hard rule that says everyone must know exactly what he or she wants to do after graduation. As a matter of fact, with so many different fields and so many new occupations being created by the rapid development of new products and services, keeping your options open for a time is probably good for you. You can try a few different kinds of jobs to see which you fit into best. Most liberal arts graduates take this route before settling into a career that they find suitable.

There is, however, a way to make your search for the right job in the right field easier. Try to match your learned skills, personality and natural aptitudes with the requirements and demands of jobs in specific fields and industries.

For example, here are a few questions you should ask yourself, matched up with job types.

1. Do I prefer working with my hands: assembling, building, repairing?
2. Do I prefer working with my mind: teaching, organizing, analyzing, solving, administering?
3. Do I prefer working alone: bookkeeping, accounting, researching, writing?
4. Do I like to work with people: selling, training, teaching, advising, consulting?
5. Would I like to help society: fund raising, social service, consumer affairs, health care?

6. Do I like to work with ideas: advertising, publishing, architecture, art?
7. Do I like power and authority: law enforcement, civil service?
8. Do I like to influence people: public relations, journalism, teaching, broadcasting?
9. Do I crave recognition: politics, theater, writing?

You get the idea. In deciding what you want to do, you should carefully consider what you want to get out of your work in addition to money.

It's an accepted fact that people do their best at work they enjoy and from which they derive the most satisfaction.

Where Would You Like to Work?

At one time, almost everyone began his or her working career within a few miles of home. This has changed radically for the generations born after World War II. Today, no city in the United States is more than six hours from any other by air. Business and industry have moved into all parts of the country, offering equal opportunities nationwide, and an affluent middle class can take more financial risks.

All of these factors have increased the mobility of young people who now move about in a way that would have shocked their grandparents.

If you think you would prefer to work in another city for any reason—climate, environment, social—start your job search there. Keep in mind, however, that while smaller cities may offer a more comfortable life-style, they contain less business activity than bigger cities. Cities in the South and Southwest, popularly known as the Sunbelt, are currently enjoying popularity, but this will eventually lead to a saturation level in terms of job availability that will cancel any advantages over a period of time.

Product or Service?

After you decide what you want to do and in what part of the country you want to do it, you must still decide what type of job you want and in what type of company. Do you want a company that manufactures, distributes or sells a product or one which performs a service? Whether this matters to you at all is a personal choice, but there are some statistics that may influence your decision.

Since 1948 the number of people employed in service industries has steadily increased. Today people employed in these areas account for a major portion of the total work force. Here are some of the services now provided by companies, large and small:

> finance and accounting—insurance—legal—personnel—management consulting—maintenance and repair—education—advertising—public relations—arts—entertainment—transportation—social service—health care—systems and procedures—electronic data processing—labor relations.

Don't think that because an organization is involved in providing services rather than automobiles, breakfast cereals, television sets or gasoline, that it does not make money. As a matter of fact, many giant service corporations make considerably higher profits because they have relatively little investment in machinery, real estate, raw materials and plant facilities.

Not-for-Profit

In your travels around the job market, you will run into firms who refer to themselves as nonprofit or not-for-profit organizations. Examples include colleges and universities, many hospitals, religious organizations, parochial schools, fundraising organizations, trade associations, medical, scientific and cultural foundations, health care organizations, labor unions, public radio and television stations and some publishing enterprises. Don't be fooled by the term "nonprofit." It simply means there are no "owners" to profit from the business. These can be very substantial organizations with big budgets. In fact, many have incomes comparable to the largest profit-making corporations.

In order to compete with industry for talent, nonprofit organizations have to pay good salaries and benefits, although at the top levels of management, big corporations generally do outrun the nonprofit sector.

There is a wide range of nonprofit activities. If you are turned off by big business (or small business), you can choose from a variety of nonprofit organizations to suit your temperament and needs. However, don't think that because an organization does not have to show a profit or pay stockholder dividends, that it offers more stability to its employees. The opposite is often true. Private donations, government grants and membership dues often dry up—and not only during bad economic times. Firings are just as common as in profit-making businesses.

There is another important point to keep in mind when choosing between business and nonprofit companies. There seems to be a mutual reluctance between the two activities to hire from the other side. People who work in nonprofit organizations for any length of time may find the doors closed when they try to move to a business position. Employers feel that because they are not profit-oriented, such organizations do not have the proper respect for the "value of the dollar" and that this attitude is reflected in their employees' work and spending habits. This is particularly true for those who have worked in the public sector and want to make a change to private enterprise.

Unfortunately this kind of thinking has been reinforced by the well-publicized waste of public funds by government, quasi-governmental agencies and some private organizations. Deservedly or not, any period of employment with a nonprofit organization makes the transition to a position in business more difficult. It also works the other way. Employers and managers feel more comfortable with those whose experience is similar to their own.

Whatever segment you choose, product or service, the techniques of effective job hunting are the same.

Large Company or Small?

There is still another choice before you. Should you work for a large company or a small one? Don't shrug this off as a minor consideration in your job hunt. It could be a key decision affecting your future and your life-style.

Here are a few of the more important pluses and minuses in each kind of company.

Large Company—Advantages

- Greater fringe benefits
- Opportunity to advance further
- Prestige makes future moves easier
- Opportunity to make contacts with experts in your field
- Company paid tuition benefits
- Greater job security with an industry leader
- Superior retirement and pension plans
- Formal training programs help you learn the business

Large Company—Disadvantages

- Stiffer competition for advancement
- Political maneuvering and back-biting among fellow-employees
- Greater possibilities for heavy travel and relocation
- A small cog in a large wheel situation for employee
- More chance of getting pigeon-holed in a dead-end department
- Loss of individuality and decision-making opportunities
- Mergers of large firms may result in lay-offs

Small Company—Advantages

- Opportunity to participate in more diversified activities
- Chance to learn faster
- Faster growth possibility in successful new company
- Opportunity to work closer with top management
- Greater chance to express your creativity
- Recognition from the top for accomplishments
- More informal relationships with associates and supervisors

Small Company—Disadvantages

- Competition from larger firms can affect profitability of company
- Lack of adequate capital can hinder growth
- Fringe benefits such as pension plans and stock options are limited
- Nepotism more likely, which can prevent advancement
- Errors in judgment or bad decisions reach top management quickly. Few cushions between you and the boss

Although as a first-time job-hunter you should seriously consider the arguments for and against a large or small company, this should not be your only consideration in choosing a firm. Small companies have been known to grow into big ones, and those who joined them in their infancy have reached top offices in record time.

On the other hand, corporate giants have been known to dive into oblivion for many reasons—poor economy, mergers, incompetent management and fraud, among others.

Also keep in mind that a big firm usually has a big public relations department whose job, among others, is to impress present and prospective stockholders, while the small ones who may enjoy better management, good reputations and high profits remain outside the public eye.

Don't agonize too much over the size of the firm. It is your first job and chances are you will have many more in your career. Overanalyzing a potential employer can be counterproductive. The important thing is to get on somebody's payroll and to learn something about the business. Don't be too anxious to jump at the first company that offers you a job, but don't worry if the firm doesn't meet every one of your requirements. Most will not. Job applicants who set extra rigid standards that prevent them from accepting reasonable, although less than perfect job offers, find themselves among the unemployed far longer than those who are more flexible.

What Are Your Major Interests?

Most people spend more time thinking about choosing their clothes or their cars than about choosing their careers. That's one of the reasons why so many get locked into unsatisfactory and unfulfilling jobs. In later life, when they try to change, it is too late. The trick is to try to choose the occupation that reflects your aptitudes, likes and dislikes, talents and preferences.

Obviously this is much easier said than done. If everyone could spend their lives doing what they enjoy doing, and make lots of money doing it, career satisfaction would be the rule instead of the exception.

It is difficult to be successful in a career you dislike. Professional sports figures, entertainers and best-selling novelists in all probability love what they do and love even more the big money that comes with it. But even if you are not Reggie Jackson, Elizabeth Taylor or Irving Wallace, you can still try to find something pleasant and potentially lucrative to do with your life. If you happen to be the son of a wealthy Arab sheik, you already have a good start, but if you are starting out with slightly fewer advantages, you need to give careful thought as to what you want to do to earn your living.

Even if you have already chosen your career, it can pay to review your reasons for doing so. What you think you might like to do doesn't always agree with what you are capable of doing, and that's where a lot of beginners go wrong.

This is particularly true if you really don't know what kind of work you want to do.

If you really want to determine in a more scientific manner in what career you would have the best chances of success, you should seek professional career guidance and aptitude testing. Your school counselor can recommend a source, or you can inquire at your local U.S. Employment Service office, where there are testing programs available to veterans and nonveterans alike. Private testing organizations in your community can also administer tests to help you make career decisions. These can be found in your local Yellow Pages.

But remember, in the last analysis, your choice to be successful must be a combination of both what you want to do and what you can do.

Summing Up

- Finding a job is full-time work.
- Learn to cope with rejection.
- Keep your self-confidence.
- Time is money—use it wisely.
- Keep your eye on the real world.
- Ask yourself what you would like to do and why.
- Keep an open mind but don't be a window-shopper when choosing a career.
- Choose the geographical area in which you would like to settle before starting your search.
- Product or service—you have a choice.
- Large companies vs. small—where would you be happier?
- Don't look for the "perfect" first job—it probably doesn't exist.
- Can't decide what to do? Get career guidance.

2
It's Always Later Than You Think

Time not only marches on: it will march right over you if you let it. No one has yet figured out a way to get more than twenty-four hours out of every day. Knowing how to use those twenty-four hours is what separates the winners from the losers.

There is nothing that consumes time faster than looking for a job. First you have to locate a company that has an opening. That can take from a few weeks to a few months . . . depending on the job market, your qualifications and how lucky you happen to be. If you are answering a blind help-wanted ad in the newspaper where a letter is necessary, you have to wait for the employer to respond, which sometimes never happens. You are also at the mercy of the U.S. Postal Service, which hasn't won any medals for speed since the Pony Express. That's another week or so lost. Then you may hit the jackpot and be invited in for an interview. That's great, but look at the date—next week. You appear on time. The interview seems to go well (at least from your standpoint), and you are told to go home and wait for a call. In many cases, if you take this advice seriously, be sure and lay in a good supply of potato chips. It may take some time.

If the interview really did go well, you may be asked to come back—not for a job, but for another interview. Add another week or two.

Of course, there is always the possibility that you can get a job the first week out. There's also the possibility that you can win a million dollars in the lottery. The odds are about the same. In case you're not that lucky, here are a few tips on how to make your time work for you.

Set Quotas

The most effective way to efficiently use time to accomplish all your job-hunting activities is to set quotas for yourself. For instance, you know the things you have to do: answer ads, write letters, register with employment agencies, do research, send out résumés, contact companies, make telephone calls, etc. Where do you start? Without some organization you will find yourself jumping from one activity to another and not really doing justice to any of them.

Here's how successful salespeople handle what is essentially the same time problem. Faced with a long list of prospects to call on—old customers to be serviced, new firms to be contacted, telephone calls, follow-up letters, complaints and a myriad of other details that have to be accomplished within a limited time—the successful salesperson simply divides the day into manageable segments and devotes each to specific activities. You can do the same. In addition to blocking out time for each activity, a good salesperson also sets a minimum number of calls he or she makes on prospects and customers every day, and sticks to it.

This may sound like a lot of silly regimentation to the inexperienced, but look at the mathematics. Setting a quota to contact five prospects a day doesn't sound like much, but if done conscientously it means 25 calls a week, 100 calls a month, 1200 calls a year. You can see the possibilities. Each individual can set different quotas depending on the time needed for each activity. But the system is only effective if the quota is met. It can be adjusted up or down as time goes on until the right mix is set. The key is self-discipline. It's easy to set a quota. The tough part is forcing yourself to meet it.

Undisciplined salespeople can be spotted easily. They're the ones with briefcases, sitting on park benches, figuring out the track odds or waiting on line at the local unemployment office.

You as a job-hunter can make good use of the successful salesperson's system. For example, if you are answering help-wanted advertising in your daily newspaper, set a quota for yourself of answering ten ads a week. You will be conducting a direct-mail campaign as described in Chapter 5. Discipline yourself to write at least two letters a day. Visit at least one new employment agency every day and contact an agency with whom you are already registered once a week.

By setting quotas and meeting them, letters and résumés will go out, and telephone calls to and contacts with prospective employers will be made. Within a few weeks you will be pleasantly surprised at the cumulative effect of such a system.

A word of caution: in setting quotas, don't aim so high that you cannot accomplish what you set out to do, but make your goals high enough to keep yourself busy.

Things to Do Today

Whenever you think that there is plenty of time to do everything you would like to do, consider the fact that in an eight-hour day there are only 480 minutes. That's not much, so you will have to hustle to make the most of them. One way to organize those 480 minutes is to make a "Things to Do Today" list. Each morning, or the night before, list all the things you want to accomplish for the day ahead and try to complete each one. Don't demand too much of yourself by listing an unreasonable number of things to do. Extra long lists are rarely completed. If you have to keep moving the things you have not done over to the next morning, either your list is too long or you are a bit on the lazy side.

Keep Office Hours

Since looking for a job should be considered a full-time job in itself, pretend you are working for a tough boss who demands punctuality and hard work.

The first rule is to get in on time. This doesn't mean that you have to be out of the house every day at 9 A.M., but you should be working on something pertaining to your job search by that time. That doesn't mean working while watching the latest disasters on the morning news or listening to your favorite record.

Leisurely breakfasts and vacationlike routines are out for the duration. Write the first letter of the day, mail a résumé, call a prospect or an employment agency or go out for your first appointment.

Also, don't quit early in the afternoon because you have completed your scheduled activities by 3 P.M. Visit the public library and research some companies, or make an extra telephone call.

There's another benefit from efficient time use besides the practical one of getting a job sooner. It's hard not to become discouraged when you discover that your letters go unanswered and your phone is not ringing. Setting and meeting quotas for activities allows you little time to get depressed or indulge in self-pity. It's easier on your family if they don't have to see you moping around the house.

Summing Up

- Set quotas for all of your job-hunting activities.
- Discipline yourself to contact a minimum number of prospects each day.
- Organize your eight-hour day into manageable segments.
- Make a daily list of things to accomplish and keep to it.
- Spend the same hours working on a job campaign as you would on a regular job.
- Keep busy and you won't have time to get discouraged.

3

Keeping Records

Before your job hunt is successfully concluded, you will have met many people, sent out dozens of résumés and letters and made countless telephone calls. You will have also given and received information on salaries, job specifications, qualifications, dates, telephone numbers, addresses, names and titles.

In fact, enough information will flow through you to keep a small computer busy. You will have long telephone conversations, interviews and discussions. Failing to keep accurate records can get you into trouble and even cause you to lose a job opportunity.

Did you ever forget the name of someone immediately after being introduced? It has happened to everyone at one time or another. In a social setting, it is embarrassing. In an interview it can be disastrous.

To ensure install recall of important facts and figures when you need them, get a supply of 5″ × 8″ index cards. At the top of each card enter the name of the company to whom you sent your letter and résumé, or paste the want-ad you answered or the name of the employment agency you are working with. Enter every contact you have made and your impressions of the company and your interviewer. Write it all down as soon as possible, while it is still fresh in your mind. Whenever you have a call-back or want to follow up on a letter, résumé or interview, all you need do is pull out the right card and you can immediately recall all the facts, figures and impressions that you need.

Companies Keep Records—You Should Too

The value of a recall card system is most important when you are negotiating with a prospective employer. It usually takes more than one interview to get hired and in some cases four or five different interviewers get into the act. First the personnel manager or an assistant, then the head of the department in which the job exists, and perhaps a divisional manager. Then back to the personnel department and sometimes back through the mill again. Everyone along the line will be evaluating you and making copious notes about every aspect of your education and background, running up a hefty dossier on you. You will never see this record, so if you don't keep your facts straight from one interviewer to another, you are bound to get into trouble somewhere along the line.

Keeping records will give you some of the same advantages in your interviews and negotiations, so don't trust your memory. Samples of these cards follow this chapter.

11

The Résumé Referral Record

In addition to your index card file, start a résumé referral sheet (see sample below).

Every time you mail or leave a résumé with someone, whether in answer to an ad, when registering with an employment agency or at an interview, enter all the details called for on the form. This will give you an instant picture of where your résumés are, when they were sent and for what jobs. It's the best device invented for an effective follow-up.

Summing Up

- Keep daily records of all of your activities.
- Right after an interview, write down all of the facts and figures you discussed.
- Keep a written record of where you send every résumé.
- Make a separate index card for every job contact for instant recall when necessary.
- Keep a copy of every letter or note that you send out.

Date	Name and address of company	Officer and title	Position and source	REMARKS: Response, follow-up, etc.

4

The "No Experience" Résumé

How do you write a résumé of your background and experience when you have very little of each? You could write it on a very small piece of paper in large letters, or you could write your name and address across the top and leave the rest blank. Neither way really works too well, however.

As a beginner in the job market, you have a much tougher job writing a résumé than you will when you have lots of experience because you have very little to say and a big page on which to say it. But don't feel too badly. Even with meager material, you too can construct a résumé that is informative and that will get you interviews. Without filling the page with trivia, it is possible to organize your limited experience into an interesting presentation.

Plan Before You Write

Before writing the actual résumé you should have a plan or outline and know just what is going to go into it and in what sequence.

First, compile the material you need. If you are a recent college graduate, have a copy of your transcript handy. Make a list of the special courses you took in high school or any other educational institution you attended. List the summer or part-time jobs you held. Don't worry about form or format at this point. Your purpose now is to get down on paper all the things you studied, everything you have done, and your special aptitudes and interests. All of these items will be organized later when you actually start writing the résumé. When you have finished, you will have before you a rough autobiography from which you can abstract the information you will ultimately include in your résumé.

The Résumé Preparation Form

On pages 20–22 you will find the Résumé Preparation Form. This has been designed to help you write the best possible résumé by including all of the pertinent information that is required. Fill it in completely, including your name, address and telephone number. This may seem silly to you since you are certainly going to include these items in your real résumé, but you would be surprised at the number of résumés that come into offices without names and addresses, while the writers sit forlornly at silent telephones and empty mailboxes wondering why nobody is interested in them.

Be sure to include your age or date of birth. It is illegal for a prospective employer to ask you your age, but there is no law preventing you from volunteering it. Employers feel more comfortable when they know an applicant's age, and you have nothing to gain by concealing it.

What You Would Like to Do—Your Objective

The next item on the form is your job objective. This should be included even though you may not have yet really decided what it is. At this stage you may be considering several options. This situation is not uncommon among new job-hunters, especially those who have a liberal arts education or have taken courses that have little practical application in the business world. For instance, your proficiency in deciphering Egyptian hieroglyphics or in theatrical stage management is not going to thrill an interviewer for a company that makes breakfast cereals. The same applies, in some degree, to studies in political science, history and psychology. And don't try to impress an employer with your interest in elective subjects such as belly dancing, yoga, backpacking and winemaking, unless of course you are looking for a job as a belly-dancing, yoga-practicing, winemaking mountain climber—a field with relatively limited possibilities.

In listing your job objectives, do not make the mistake a lot of trainees do of projecting your entire life's goals in a first résumé. It should be a concise statement, reflecting your short- or medium-term goals. Avoid phrases like "leading to an executive position" or "to become a member of top management." These are both presumptuous and vague. And speaking of vagueness, one memorable résumé contained the following heading: "To be constructively in sequence with defined responsibility and staff functional purpose within management."

Other descriptions to avoid are those that are too general and really mean nothing. For example: "To join a firm that will offer a challenging opportunity and a future." Who doesn't want that? "To obtain a position where I can work with people." With the exception of lion tamers, everybody works with people.

On the other hand, don't get too specific. You may talk yourself out of an interview if your objective appears too rigid. For example: "To obtain a position where I can use my interest in international political affairs." The Secretary of State's job is already filled.

Another type of job objective that can work against you is the one that covers too much territory and indicates that you would do anything to get a job. "Objective: Position as a communications specialist or any other interesting position." "Position in sales, administration, purchasing or office management." That sounds too desperate.

You could write a new résumé for each job opening and tailor your objective specifically to it. It's done frequently, but it requires many hours at the typewriter and continuous revisions to fit each position. It's also time-consuming and unnecessary. You can compose an objective that does not restrict your options and, at the same time, has enough direction to interest an employer.

For example:

"Objective: A career in finance or a finance-related field, with the opportunity to advance to a responsible position."

"Objective: Entry-level position in marketing, leading to product management responsibilities."

"Objective: Seeking a position with a firm offering on-the-job training in marketing and advertising."

"Objective: An administrative position where I can use my office skills to become a valuable executive assistant."

What You Have Learned—Your Education

Your education should be listed directly following your objective. At this stage of your career, it is the only thing you have going for you and it will constitute most of your résumě.

Start with the dates of your school attendance, followed by the name of the school and any degrees, diplomas or certificates you earned. Indicate your major and minor subjects. It's not necessary to show all the courses you took—just those that have some bearing on the kind of job you are after.

Forget your A's in physical training or gourmet cooking. Your mother was probably impressed by the fact that you made the squash team or did the twenty two-mile marathon in 3 hours, 14 minutes, but it will only make a prospective employer yawn. Hobbies fall into the same category. Employers are not particularly thrilled at your competence in surfing. Your interest in cats or antique cars is very nice, but it is of doubtful value to a reader of your résumé.

Do, however, list any of your extracurricular activities such as working on your school newspaper or magazine, membership in a professional (not social) fraternity or sorority, student teaching, special projects or laboratory work.

If you graduated in the upper 10 percent of your class, say so. Otherwise, don't mention grades on the résumé. If you earned any honors, if you made the dean's list or were awarded any prizes or citations for scholastic achievement, include them. Don't be too bashful to blow your own horn, but try to retain a measure of modesty. You are not quite ready for the "Oh, how wonderful I am" résumé until you show some tangible, on-the-job results.

If you have had any supplementary schooling, such as attending night school, correspondence courses, trade or professional association seminars or applicable military service courses, list those. Every little bit helps when you're a raw recruit.

What You Have Done So Far—Your Experience

The next part of the résumé is for your experience. Students who were gainfully employed during summers or part-time while attending school are in a preferred position when it comes to being considered for a job. The best kind of summer employment is as an intern with a firm doing the kind of work for which you are being trained.

If you do not qualify or were not in an internship program, any kind of supplementary or summer job is preferable to none at all.

While you are in school, you should try for a job as a salesperson, an administrative assistant or some work that will involve you in duties having an association with business, no matter how menial. Those whose part-time or summer experience was in a business setting have a bit of an edge from the corporate viewpoint.

If you have not been fortunate enough to have a business position but have worked, for example, as a waiter or a baby-sitter, you may want to list the date and the job. It's not necessary in this case to describe the job in detail.

What You Can Offer an Employer

In terms of experience, you can offer very little to an employer. But you can offer him or her hard work and loyalty. These simple expressions and others like them woven into a résumé can do you no harm.

Accentuate the Positive

Never include negative information in a résumé. Put your natural modesty aside temporarily. For instance, if you dropped out of school, don't say "I only attended for a short time" or "I was not able to get a degree." Turn your dropping out for whatever reason into a positive action.

"I want to enter the business world now to get experience and intend to continue my education in the evening."

"I completed my third year at New York University, but due to financial difficulties, I was forced to withdraw. I intend to pursue a degree at night."

Don't use negative statements such as: "Although I am not a college graduate . . ." or "I have not had any experience in your field, but . . .".

Employers know you are a beginner. Don't make excuses for your lack of experience or education or say or write anything that sounds like a plea for mercy. An employer knows he or she is taking a risk with a beginner. Don't try to convince him or her that this is correct.

Miscellaneous or Personal Information

This should be the last heading on your résumé. It is used to provide all of the information that doesn't fit into the rest of the résumé but which you want to include.

YOUR AGE

The law says you don't have to give your age, but put it in anyway. You are young and your age is in your favor.

MARITAL STATUS

Again, the law says that an employer cannot use your marital status for the purpose of determining whether or not to hire you, and in most states it is illegal to include it on an application form or in an interview. However, no law prevents you from volunteering this information. If you are single, it will be to your advantage to state that fact. Some employers feel that married applicants may not be willing to travel or relocate when necessary. Also there is a feeling that a single employee would not feel the same financial pressure as a married one. This is especially true of a person starting a first job where the salary is moderate.

TRAVEL AND RELOCATION

Many medium or large firms are involved in national and international business and have offices and facilities in different parts of the United States and the world. It's a good idea to say that you are willing to relocate and travel. You may not be too keen on doing either at this point in your life, but it is something companies like to hear.

Even if you feel strongly about unlimited travel and think you would like to stay in your hometown forever, wait until you are involved in an interview before you commit yourself. You may want to change your mind when you hear more about the job, and you want to leave yourself as many options as possible when you are starting out.

YOUR HEALTH

Although it appears on many résumés, it's not necessary to state that you are strong, robust and in good health. Employers know that if you weren't, you wouldn't admit it. This also applies to permanent disabilities. You would not knowingly apply for a job that you were sure you could not perform physically. But for any other job, telling an employer (on your résumé) that you have a disability is like waving a red flag in front of a bull. There are laws that make it illegal to discriminate against an individual because of disability. If you are disabled, the interview is the time to discuss the matter.

REFERENCES

All you need say is "references furnished on request." Nobody in their right mind gives a bad reference, so it really doesn't carry weight on a résumé. Since you have little or no formal work experience, performance references are not available, and employers don't put much credence on recommendations from school counselors, favorite professors or your Uncle Morris.

Résumé "No-Nos"

RACE, RELIGION, NATIONAL ORIGIN

They are completely irrelevant and no information alluding to them should appear. Because of the pressure on corporations by equal opportunity laws, minority applicants sometimes identify themselves as such, thinking it will enhance their chances for an interview, especially with companies doing business with the government. Under no circumstances is it proper to label yourself on your résumé as a member of any religious or racial group.

PHOTOGRAPHS

Don't include them, unless you are applying for a modeling job. If you're beautiful or handsome, including your photograph is an act of immodesty. If you're plain, it's an act of stupidity. It serves no useful purpose either way.

OFFBEAT RÉSUMÉS

They can sometimes be effective in certain fields such as advertising, public relations, graphic arts, radio and television, but mostly for those with experience.

For the majority of occupations, be conventional. Business is basically conservative—especially at the lower levels. Cleverness, cuteness and flamboyance in a résumé may get a chuckle from an employer, but those who are called in for an interview are the writers of the conventional, informative, and usually dull résumés. This is probably a commentary on our poor sense of originality, but nevertheless true.

Make It Easy to Read

Résumés should always be typed or printed on a standard $8\frac{1}{2}'' \times 11''$ sheet of paper. Undersized or oversized résumés tend to cause filing problems. Intricate folds and fancy covers add nothing to your résumé except cost. Yours should be neatly typed and contain no strikeovers, messy erasures or errors in spelling or grammar. Avoid abbreviations where possible. If English was not your strong subject or if you are a poor speller, let someone more proficient help you put your résumé in good shape. A misspelled word or a poorly constructed sentence is not always fatal, but a fussy reader might be put off.

Your résumé should fit on one page. If you have to go to a second page, review it carefully to see where you can tighten it up. You may be writing too much. Remember, you are not composing an autobiography.

Lay out your résumé so that you show lots of white space in the margins and between headings. Personnel people spend a large part of their days reading résumés. Résumés with wall-to-wall type are not going to do anyone's failing eyesight any good. Nor will they improve a prospective employer's disposition.

Personnel managers and assistants have refined their skimming processes to a science. In large companies where résumés come in by the hundreds every day, the task of reading them is usually allocated to a minor personnel official who cannot possibly read every one with the care it deserves. So what they do is skim—glancing at the résumé annd extracting just enough information to determine whether it is worthy of further consideration or destined for the dead file. A résumé that looks like a solid blob of ink stands little chance of a second look.

Résumés should be single spaced with double spacing between headings and paragraphs. Underscore job titles, capitalize company names, use lots of indentations and leave margins of at least one inch at the sides and top and bottom of the page. If you go on to a second page, staple the pages together, type your name at the top left-hand side of the second page and the number 2 at the top right. In case the pages separate, your second page won't be orphaned.

After you have had your résumé typed, have it printed by offset or reproduced on a copier, using good quality bond paper.

Summing Up

- Do not begin to write a résumé without careful planning.
- Fill out the Résumé Preparation Form completely.
- Your objective—know what you want but don't get too specific. Keep your options open.
- Your education—list your degrees, diplomas, awards and pertinent extracurricular activities.

- Omit trivial elective courses that have no bearing on the kind of job you are after.
- Show all work experience while attending school, especially internships.
- Make only positive statements—never apologize for any shortcomings (imagined or real) in a résumé.
- Never refer to your race, religion or nationality.
- Keep it conventional—standard size and format.
- Make it fit on a single page.

RÉSUMÉ PREPARATION FORM (1)

NAME: _____

ADDRESS: _____

TELEPHONE: _____ _____
                (home)   (messages)

OBJECTIVE OR JOB TITLE: _____

_____

_____

_____

EDUCATION:

High School: _____
(List only if you are not a college graduate, or if it was a trade school or offered specialized business or technical courses.)

College or University _____

_____

Dates of attendance _____ Degree _____

Major area of studies _____

Minor area of studies _____

Grade average (major) _____ (overall) _____

Extracurricular activities, professional fraternities, sororities, organizations, study groups, etc.

_____

_____

_____

Work-study programs, internships, positions in school, etc.

_____

_____

_____

RÉSUMÉ PREPARATION FORM (2)

WORK EXPERIENCE:

List all jobs held—part-time, full-time, summer, internships.

Dates of employment (month and year) _____

Name of company _____

Address _____

Products or services _____

Brief description of your duties _____

_____

Dates of employment _____

Name of company _____

Address _____

Product or services _____

Brief description of your duties _____

Dates of employment _____

Name of company _____

Address _____

Product or services _____

Brief description of your duties _____

_____

MISCELLANEOUS:

Special awards, honor society memberships, citations.

_____

_____

_____

_____

RÉSUMÉ PREPARATION FORM (3)

PERSONAL:

Age: (date of birth or years) _____

Travel or relocation preferences _____
Optional information (references, marital status, military experience, etc.)

_____

_____

_____

Sample Résumés:
High School, Vocational School and
Business School Graduates

BENJAMIN COOK
1300 North 22nd Street
Evansville, IN   40296

(317) 555-3487

JUNIOR DRAFTSMAN

EDUCATION

1976 - 1981   Walther High School
                   Indianapolis, IN
                   General Diploma

1980 - 1982   Donovan Technical Institute
                   Evansville, IN
                   Evening Courses
                   Drafting
                   Basic Electronics
                   Geometry
                   Trigonometry
                   Basic Physics
                   Technical Drawing
                   Schematics

EXPERIENCE

Part-time   Electronic Services, Inc.
while attending   1400 Bovier Street
high school   Evansville, IN
and Donovan
Institute   General helper for electromechanical
                   engineering design company. Prepared
                   work schedules, purchased supplies
                   and material for drafting room. Did
                   lettering and simple line work under
                   direction of draftsmen.

                   Sanford Parts and Equipment Co.
                   Evansville, Indiana

                   Office Assistant - Kept job orders,
                   purchased office supplies. Maintained
                   customers relations over the telephone.
                   Drove company delivery truck.

PERSONAL   Age: 20
                   Marital status: single
                   Health: Excellent - no physical disabilities
                   Own car

RESUME

Nancy Fergusen
18 Columbia Heights
Brooklyn, NY 11224

(212) 555-8795

OBJECTIVE
Position as Office Assistant
Where I Can Use My Clerical
    and Typing Skills

EDUCATION
Henry Clay High School
Bronx, New York
Graduated June 1981

Ryder Secretarial School
New York, NY
Currently Attending (evenings)

Course subjects:
    Typing
    Business Machines Operation
    Business English
    Speedwriting
    Basic Bookkeeping

EXPERIENCE

September 1981
to July 1982
Roth Brothers, Inc. (Stationery)
382 Park Avenue South
New York, NY 10012

Clerk/Typist and general office
assistant. Also handled switch-
board when receptionist was out
and helped sales personnel with
records and itineraries.

Summers
1980 and 1981
Part-time employment while attending high
school in administration office; file
clerk, typist and messenger.

PERSONAL
Born March 5, 1963
Marital Status: Single
Hobbies: Painting, Photography

<u>R E S U M E</u>

JAMES CARLEY, JR.
1261 East 181st Street
(212) 555-6789   Bronx, New York 10453

OBJECTIVE   Position in Word Processing or Photocomposition

SKILLS   MTST/SC
WANG Word Processor
IBM MAG CARD A
IBM MAG CARD II
COMPUGRAPHIC IV - Phototype
IBM Electronic Composer
EDITWRITER 7500
Typing: 70 w.p.m.

EDUCATION   Commercial High School
New York, NY - Diploma Graduate 1981

Courses: Basic Computer Technology
Phototype Composing Machines
Word Processing Procedures and Equipment
Typing and Speedwriting

EXPERIENCE   <u>June 1981 - Present</u>
Continental Corporation
521 Fifth Avenue
New York, NY 10017

Word Processor and Phototypsetter
(Evening shift - 3 to 11 P.M.)

<u>June - September 1980</u>
Allen Printing Co.
46-82 Sutphin Boulevard
Rego Park, NY 11340

Production Assistant and Proof Press Operator
(Summer position)

<u>PERSONAL</u>   Age: 19

Marital Status: Single

Driver's License

RESUME

Joan R. Eisenman
1251 Raritan Avenue
Bay Shore, NY 11705

(516) 555-4587

JOB OBJECTIVE   Assistant Bookkeeper

EDUCATION   DeWitt Clinton High School
                       Bronx, New York
                       General Diploma - 1981

                       Lincoln Business School
                       New York, NY - 1982

                       Major Subjects
                       Basic Accounting
                       Typing
                       Credit Procedures
                       General Office Administration
                       Basic Computer Language

EXPERIENCE   RICHARD INDUSTRIES, INC.
June 1982 to   1475 Walton Avenue
present   Bronx, New York

                       Part-time position with this manufacturer
                       of electronic games. Receptionist and
                       clerk. Handled customer relations, billing
                       and typing. Kept inventory of office
                       supplies. Assisted sales manager in
                       preparation of travel itineraries of sales
                       personnel.

OFFICE SKILLS   Type 50 words per minute
                       Operate desk calculator
                       Knowledge of NCR billing machine
                       Experienced with monitor board
                       Knowledge of accounts receivables and
                         payables bookkeeping
                       Bank reconciliations

PERSONAL   20 years of age

                       Single

                       Available for immediate employment

SANDRA COOPER
1625 Main Street
Rye, NY   10645
(914) 555-3968

OBJECTIVE:
    To become associated with a law firm in the capacity
    of a paralegal assistant.

EDUCATION:
    1975 - 1979
    James Madison High School, New York, NY
    Commercial Course
    Subjects included typing, shorthand, commercial law,
    bookkeeping, basic word processing.

    1981 - 1982
    Metropolitan Business School, New York, NY
    Paralegal studies program
    Awarded Certificate of Distinction in Paralegal
    studies. Intensive, in-depth program that included
    office management, legal research, estate administration,
    procedures for the probate of wills and office
    memorandums drafting.

WORK EXPERIENCE:
    August 1979 - 1980
    R.H. MACY COMPANY, New York, NY
    Position: Part-time salesperson
    Responsibilities included: handling of cash and charge
    transactions, assisting customers in the selection of
    merchandise, arranging and maintaining merchandise
    on the selling floor and inventory control activities.

    April 1978 - July 1979
    OFFICE OF THE DISTRICT ATTORNEY, Brooklyn, NY
    Position: General clerk
    Responsibilities included collating of legal
    materials, typing of legal documents, correspondence
    and telephone contact with other legal agencies.

    March 1976 - August 1977
    MUSEUM OF MODERN ART BOOKSHOP, New York, NY
    Position: Part-time salesperson
    Responsibilities included sales transactions,
    customer assistance, inventory counts, filing, typing
    and general office and store duties.

PERSONAL:
    Age 21
    Available for immediate employment
    References furnished on request

Community College Graduates

R E S U M E

Brian Davis
234 W. 21st Street
New York, NY 10036

(212) 555-6730

JOB OBJECTIVE

Position as photo assistant in a photographic studio,
        advertising agency or corporation

EDUCATION

September 1981   New York City Community College
to May 1982   New York, NY
                   AAS: Photography

                   Courses of Study
                   Fundamentals of Photography
                   Commercial Photography
                   Portrait Illustration and Lighting
                   Color Studio Techniques
                   Ektacolor Printing
                   Laboratory Procedures
                   Photographic Chemicals

EXPERIENCE

June 1982 to   Ted Richstone Photo Studio
February 1982   New York, NY
                   Responsibilities: Black-and-white product
                   shots with an 8" x 10" view camera for
                   catalog illustration and advertising.
                   Darkroom duties included developing,
                   printing and mounting.

February 1982   Lawrence Photo Studios   (Part-time)
to Present   New York, NY
                   Responsibilities: Lab Assistant.
                   Develop and print black and white and
                   color photographs. Work with clients
                   in setting up photo sessions on the
                   premises and on location. Order
                   supplies and keep billing records.

MISCELLANEOUS

Knowledge of all camera formats through
8" x 10" and 11" x 14"
Familiar with most widely used strobe
equipment
22 years old - single

CAROL HART
1261 West 2nd Street
Kansas City, MO   63476

Telephone: (314) 555-6954

Employment Objective: An entry-level secretarial
position that will afford opportunities
to progress within the company.

Education: Riley Community College
Kansas City, KS
Candidate for Associate in Arts
Degree, June 1982 - Business

Subjects:
Typing
Shorthand
Business Machines
Bookkeeping
English
Word Processing Techniques
Computer Language

Central High School
Kansas City, MO
General Course
Diploma 1980

Work History:
June 1980 to   Petco Machine Tool Co.
September 1980   1475 Grand Avenue
Kansas City, MO
Job Title: Sales Clerk
Maintained salesmen's records and
production control records. Kept
inventory sheets of raw materials.

June 1979 to   Levin Realty Co.
September 1979   12 W. Nyatt Street
Kansas City, MO
Job Title: Clerk Typist
Typed and filed sales orders. Kept
rent receipt books, arranged
appointments for sales people.

Extracurricular Activities:
Student Senate Secretary
Vice-President of Sophomore Class
Honor Roll

Personal: Single, 21 years old
Have car

College and Graduate School Graduates

SARAH R. COPELAND
1461 Albany Street
Phoenix, AZ 85282

(602) 555-3324

OBJECTIVE	Entry-level Management Training Program/Sales
EDUCATION	University of California at Davis B.S. degree, Business Administration June 1982 Deans List, GPA 3.9 (4.0 major) Gamma Phi Honor Society Business Management Association Honor Society
SPECIALIZED COURSES	Introduction to Computers Economics Financial Analysis Marketing Research Sales Management Psychology
EXPERIENCE	Summer 1981 Franklin, March & Radcliffe, Davis, CA Administrative Assistant - revised filing system, posted accounts payables and receivables, maintained sales commission records. Summer 1980 Southwest Office Services, Phoenix, AZ (Temporary Agency) Handled correspondence for Sales Manager of Arizona Bell Telephone Company. Also performed duties of general office assistant, arranging reservations, ordering supplies and writing reports. Summer 1979 United Freight, Inc., Phoenix, AZ Claims department - handled office details, typing and filing. Assisted in the processing of claims.
SOCIETIES	Marketing Society University Travel and Film Committees Arizona Olympics Committee Photography Club
PERSONAL	Age: 24 - single Willing to travel and/or relocate

MARY ROCKLAND
165 Third Street
Jersey City, NJ 07123

(201) 555-4367

JUNIOR COPYWRITER

EDUCATION: Rutgers University - Summa Cum Laude
                    B.A., 1982   Major: English
                                    Minor: Psychology

EXTRACURRICULAR: Reporter and advertising manager on college
                    paper
                    Member of debating team

EXPERIENCE:
June 1981 to   Intern with Consolidated Advertising Agency,
September 1981   420 Fifth Avenue, New York, NY

                    Worked as general assistant in copy department
                    under direct supervision of copy chief.
                    Principal duties were typing and checking
                    copy, filing, relief receptionist and
                    switchboard operator.

                    Was permitted to attend several copy
                    conferences, and finally wrote original copy
                    for two small food accounts. Both accepted -
                    one appeared in Ladies Home Journal and the
                    other was used in a direct mail piece.

June 1980 to   Market Research Interviewer
September 1980   Consumer Analysis, Jersey City, NJ
                    Surveys conducted under variety of conditions
                    among various consumer groups. Helped compile
                    data from one study to form basis for
                    national research project on the consumer
                    spending potential for household appliances.

                    While in college, was advertising manager for
                    college newspaper; increased regular
                    advertisers from seven to eighteen over a
                    period of three years, eliminating the deficit
                    in our budget and enabling us to make a down
                    payment on the purchase of badly needed
                    equipment for the newspaper office.

PERSONAL DATA: Age 22
                    Marital Status: Single
                    Available for immediate employment

                    References furnished on request

R E S U M E

Victor Belson
1425 Washington Place
Indianapolis, IN 52182

(812) 555-4598

EMPLOYMENT
OBJECTIVE: A responsible entry-level position in
               marketing leading to product management
               responsibilities.

EDUCATION: Master of Business Administration 1980-1982
               Ohio State University
               Major: Marketing

               Master's degree field project:
               Conducted a marketing survey for a nationally
               known corporation.

               Evaluated and analyzed regional demographics
               for forecasting share of market and to
               determine wholesalers' and dealers'
               motivations, consumer attitudes and competitors'
               share of the market.

               Bachelor of Science   1976 - 1980
               Indiana State University
               Major: Economics

EXPERIENCE: Midwestern Savings Bank   1974 - 1976
               18 W. 36th Street
               Indianapolis, IN

               Assistant to Life Insurance Officer - Advised
               customers on savings bank life insurance
               policies. Received and processed applications.
               Answered inquiries by telephone and by mail.

               Franklin Real Estate Co., Inc.
               1230 Main Street
               Indianapolis, IN

               Employed three summers during college as
               Assistant to Office Manager.

ACTIVITIES: Active volunteer for local chapter of the
               Muscular Dystrophy Association.

PERSONAL
DATA: Age 25 - Single - Can travel and/or relocate

R E S U M E

GEORGE TAYLOR
2701 West Highway
Baltimore, MD 48670

(301) 555-6878 - Home

(301) 555-2900 - Messages

ADVERTISING TRAINEE

OBJECTIVE
Seeking an entry-level position in the
advertising department of a company
offering on-the-job training in the field
of advertising and sales promotion.

EDUCATION
Washington & Lee University
Lexington, VA
B.S., Business Management - February 1982

Major: Advertising
Minor: Marketing

SCHOLASTIC
ACHIEVEMENTS
Dean's List - Two Semesters
Graduated upper ten percent of class

SCHOOL
ACTIVITIES
Member Advertising Club
Editor of Student News Magazine

JOB
EXPERIENCE
Summers 1980 - 1982

ELMER BRADLEY ADVERTISING AGENCY
1428 Main Street
Baltimore, MD

Traffic Assistant - Worked under the production
manager of the agency participating in all
aspects of traffic, plus general clerical
and administrative duties.

PERSONAL
Single

Date of birth: April 6, 1957

Available for travel

Willing to relocate

Served two years in the Maryland National Guard

```
                    LAWRENCE CORCORAN
                     46-12 Bay Parkway
                    Brooklyn, NY 11321
                     (212) 555-4389
```

JOB OBJECTIVE

A position in computer programming where I can apply my education and skills in achieving a rewarding career.

EDUCATION

September 1981 to June 1982

PRATT INSTITUTE OF DATA PROCESSING AND PROGRAMMING - DIPLOMA PROGRAM
Twelve undergraduate credits in Business Application Programming.

LANGUAGES: COBOL, BAL/OS
HARDWARE: IBM 370-4341 OS/VS
SOFTWARE: RSTS-E VERSION 7 OS

Instruction received in problem analysis, flowcharting, debugging, testing, record and file design, accessing techniques, structured programming, and operating systems concepts. Detailed programming done in COBOL and ASSEMBLER.

Projects: Payroll, sales analysis using table handling applications and updating of files using design and accessing techniques.

October 1980 to May 1981

CITY UNIVERSITY OF NEW YORK/QUEENS COLLEGE
6 Credits: FORTRAN and PASCAL.

August 1976 to June 1980

THE STATE UNIVERSITY OF NEW YORK AT ALBANY
B.S. BUSINESS ADMINISTRATION
Overall G.P.A. - 3.4

Major: Marketing/Management - Minor: Economics

WORK EXPERIENCE

August 1980 to April 1981

E.F. LAMSTON TIME SHARING, INC.
New York, NY

Liaison between programmers and management
Communicated user needs to programmers
Evaluated report programs to in-house system
Trained personnel in computer operations
Assisted media buyers on projects requiring
  use of computerized reports
Coordinated study that lead to a more
  efficient cost-accounting system.

SUMMER WORK

1977 - 1979

HUMAN RESOURCES ADMINISTRATION
New York, NY

Accounts Payable Clerk

MISCELLANEOUS

Age - 24 - single

5
Classified Advertising

The U.S. Department of Labor reported in a recent survey that 60 percent of the employers who were polled hired through classified advertising. Obviously, this is a prime source of jobs. It is also the quickest and easiest way to assess the job market in your community.

When the economy is good, the classified section of your newspaper is thick. When there is a decrease in business activity for any reason, the number of help-wanted pages slips accordingly. If you want to determine the general state of the economy in any area, you can get a pretty good idea by charting the fluctuations in its help-wanted advertising.

One prestigious business research organization, the Conference Board, does exactly that, and its reports are used by the federal government and business in compiling economic indexes.

Help-wanted ads are important to you in another way. The demand for people in your particular occupation is indicated by the number of appropriate openings published each week. This obviously has a direct bearing on your chances for a job in your chosen field and it can also influence your salary expectations.

For instance, if you are an aspiring accountant and you see that there are two or three solid columns of accounting jobs listed, you know that your specialty is in short supply. Since you have a wide choice of openings, you can be more selective in choosing the company and be more independent when it comes to salary demands.

Conversely, if only a few positions appear over a period of time, you know you will have a problem. All the accounting candidates in your area will be competing for a limited number of openings. Employers will have a buyer's market and can get the best applicants at the lowest salary.

How to Use Classified Advertising

The first thing you will need is strong eyesight. Lacking that, get yourself a magnifying glass. Classified advertising managers are ingenious. They have succeeded in reducing the size of the typeface to the point where they can get fifty words or more in one square inch of newspaper. A single classified page in a full-size newspaper can contain as many as 150 or more individual help-wanted ads. And if that's not bad enough, advertisers, in order to save space and money, have developed a whole new language of abbreviations that sometimes border on the unintelligible. For example:

"LIBR-MLS   \$16–17K   F/P
Ref Libn. Adv/mktg lib. Rel exp w/anal skl.
Divers. 40 wpm type, gd ben. A&S Employment Agency.

Translation: Librarian—Master's Degree in Library Science. Salary: \$16,000 to \$17,000—Fee Paid. Reference librarian. Advertising and marketing library. Related experience with analytical skills. Diversified. Forty words per minute typing. Good benefits.

This is an actual advertisement taken from a newspaper and although they are not at all that vague, there are enough to make life difficult for the new jobhunter. The more you read these ads, the easier they will become to translate into English.

Once you get the knack, you will discover that some ads give you little or no information, while others promise you opportunities beyond your wildest dreams. Somewhere in between are the serious job offers. The trick is to identify and use them. Here are a few tips to help you in that direction.

Read every single ad from A to Z. Don't skip any because the first word or two don't seem to be in your field. Most newspapers alphabetize their listings by the first word in the ad, which should be the actual title of the job being offered. Through carelessness or ignorance, however, advertisers don't always do this. If you are looking for a job in the general area of finance, you may find your listing under Accounting, Banking, Finance, Wall Street, Bookkeeping, or half-a-dozen other listings.

Secretaries are listed under the categories of Administrative Assistants, Executive Secretaries or Girl/Man Friday. Under the title of Assistant may be found almost any occupation—Assistant Bookkeeper, Assistant Service Station Manager, Assistant Buyer, Assistant Advertising Manager, etc.

To compound the problem, newspapers make mistakes and your ideal job may be buried in the wrong category because someone in the composing department hit the wrong key.

By reading all of the ads over a period of time, you will get a general picture of the job situation in your area. You will see which occupations are in demand and which are not. You will notice which employment agencies seem to offer the better jobs. More important, you will get an idea of salaries being offered for different jobs at different levels.

As you read the help-wanted ads from Aardvark Hunters to Zoo Assistants, have a razor blade handy to cut out the ads in which you are interested. If you find after a while that nothing in the paper fits you, you can always use the blade to shave with.

Don't be too discriminating at this stage. Cut out every ad that looks interesting. You can reread them later in light of your qualifications and preferences.

Paste each of the clipped ads on separate 5″ × 8″ index cards. This will become your control card and will contain all transactions and dates pertaining to that particular job opening.

How to Respond

There are three categories of classified ads: those run by companies with box numbers, those run by companies with their names and addresses and those run by employment agencies. In most states where agencies are licensed, they are not permitted to use box numbers and are required to identify themselves as agencies.

Companies prefer to use box numbers for several reasons: They may not want their competition to know what kind of people they are hiring. They may not want their employees to know they are hiring. Many firms prefer to see résumés before disclosing their identity.

The disadvantages to you as an applicant are obvious. You are revealing your life history to unknown parties. If you don't receive an answer, you have no way to follow up. And if you are working and answer your own company's ad, well . . . .

Most companies do not acknowledge letters from applicants in whom they have no interest. So your letters and résumés go from the mailbox to oblivion.

Let's take each category of ad separately.

EMPLOYMENT AGENCIES

It's not a good policy to walk into an employment agency without telephoning first, unless you want to sit in a waiting room twiddling your thumbs for an hour. You will have to wait your turn to see the first available counselor who, depending on how busy he or she is, may not be able to give you the necessary time. It is better to telephone first and ask the operator to let you speak to the person handling the particular job you clipped out of the newspaper.

Next, request an appointment for a specific day and hour to discuss the job. Try to avoid answering questions about your experience and background over the telephone. Your counselor may be looking for an excuse to get rid of you if you don't meet every specification.

Tell the counselor that you would like a personal meeting. Don't make it easy for him or her to turn you down over the telephone. Having an appointment gets you out of the waiting room and into a personal meeting. Many times, no matter how urgently you request an appointment you will be turned down with instructions to mail a résumé. Don't do it. Your résumé will more than likely end up in the bottomless pit that most agencies refer to as their active files. Take it personally to the agency and tell the receptionist that Mr. or Ms. So-and-So asked you to bring in your résumé. Then ask to see the person.

Once you are sitting opposite the counselor, you can turn on your charm. When you check back with an agency after having mailed your résumé, chances are that no one there will even know who you are, let alone remember what you do. If you are there in person, you will be remembered.

COMPANIES THAT SIGN THEIR ADS

Companies that run ads and sign their names are the easiest to work with. You can research the firm by using your library, school placement office or, if publicly owned, through any stockbroker's office. Then you can decide whether or not to apply for the job. The procedure is much faster than dealing with a box number, which adds at least another week to the process.

BOX NUMBERS

There is a way of finding out the name behind the box number. It's a lot of trouble, requires a little subterfuge and may pose an ethical question for some—but it is done and it works.

Have someone you know reply to the box ad by writing a letter that exactly fits the job requirements called for. Or reply to it yourself using a fictitious name and address where you can pick up your mail. If you get an affirmative reply—and you should if you fabricated a résumé to fit the job—the reply will identify the company. If you are interested, you can contact them directly. However, you cannot let them know that you are replying to their box ad which was supposed to have kept their identity secret.

Blind ads with box numbers are the must troublesome to answer. As mentioned earlier, in most states, employment agencies are not permitted to use box numbers or any other method to disguise their identity. The rule should extend to all individuals, companies and any other organizations seeking to hire people through classified advertising.

As an applicant, you are placed in the position of having to submit your life history plus your identity to an unknown party who, for all you know, may be collecting names and résumés for purposes other than employment. It has happened before. The danger is greater if you are currently employed. You may be telling your own company that you are looking for a new job. In this case, you will be lucky if embarrassment is the only penalty.

Writing Your Letter of Application

Your letter of application is as important as your résumé. As a new job-hunter, fresh out of school, your résumé will resemble all the résumés of your contemporaries. A carefully written cover letter enhances and personalizes your résumé.

The letter should be short. It is primarily a letter of introduction. At the same time, it should convince the reader that you are a qualified, viable applicant for the job. Without repeating what is already on your résumé, point out in the letter why you think you are qualified by picking out certain specifications in the ad to which you are applying and relating it to your education and experience. The sample letters on pages 57–62 indicate how this is done.

Summing Up

- Help-wanted advertising is a good index of the state of the economy in your area.
- Reading and understanding classified advertising takes practice.
- Read every ad—don't just look for the ones in your field.
- Paste each ad you cut out on your 5″ ×8″ control card.
- When answering an ad run by an employment agency, always make an appointment. Don't mail them a résumé.
- Companies who sign their ads are your best prospects, but to cover all bases you should also reply to box ads.
- Never send a résumé without a cover letter when replying to an ad.

Decoding Classified Abbreviations

JOB TITLES

Acct	— Accountant		Htl	— Hotel
Adm	— Administrative		HVAC	— Heating, Ventilating, Air Conditioning
Adv	— Advertising			
Air	— Airlines		Indl	— Industrial
Anal	— Analyst		Ins	— Insurance
Arch	— Architect		Lab	— Laboratory
Audit	— Auditor		Libr	— Library
Atty	— Attorney		Mktg	— Marketing
Bio	— Biologist		Ofc	— Office
Bkge	— Brokerage		Opr	— Operator
Bkpr	— Bookkeeper		PT	— Part-time
Buy	— Buyer		Persl	— Personnel
CE	— Civil Engineer		Prod	— Product
Chem	— Chemist		Prodn	— Production
Circ	— Circulation		Prog	— Programmer
Clk	— Clerk		PR	— Public Relations
Coll	— College		Recpt	— Receptionist
Compt	— Comptroller		Resch	— Research
Cred	— Credit		Sls	— Sales
Dicta	— Dictaphone		Secy	— Secretary
Dftg	— Drafting		Stat	— Statistics
Dftsmn	— Draftsman		Sten	— Stenography
Econ	— Economist		Swbd	— Switchboard
Edit	— Editor		Tech	— Technical
Editl	— Editorial		Temp	— Temporary
EDP	— Electronic Data Processing		Typg	— Typing
			Traf	— Traffic
Engr	— Engineer		Tnee	— Trainee
Exec	— Executive		Tvl	— Travel
Expt	— Export		Wrse	— Warehouse
F.P.	— Fee Paid		Wrtr	— Writer

DESCRIPTIVE WORDS

Asst	— Assistant		Potl	— Potential
Bgd	— Background		ProfS	— Profit Sharing
Ben	— Benefits		Promo	— Promotion
Bon	— Bonus		Rec	— Record
Com	— Commission		Reloc	— Relocation
Dntn	— Downtown		Ret	— Retired
Exp	— Experienced		Sal	— Salary
Incen	— Incentive		Sim	— Similar
Mfg	— Manufacturing		Stud	— Student
Mdtn	— Midtown		Supv	— Supervisor
Min	— Minimum		W/	— With
Natl	— National		W/WO	— With or without
Neg	— Negotiable		Wk	— Work
Opty	— Opportunity			

6
How To Beat The Competition

A common complaint of high school and college graduates looking for their first job is that getting it is like winning the lottery—pure luck. In other words, too many people for too few jobs.

But this is true if you consider only the jobs that are out in the open—those that are advertised, listed with employment agencies and generally circulated around the placement offices of schools and colleges.

What most people don't know is that more than 75 percent of the 15 million or more jobs that turn over each year never get into the public view. They crop up in all areas, all occupations and on all levels. The one thing they have in common is that they do not go out looking for you. You have to find them.

Not very many job-hunters know about this market, and an even fewer know how to tap it. These "hidden" jobs are generally filled in three ways.

1. *Internally, within the firm.* Most sizeable companies make it a policy to circulate a job within the firm before going outside to fill it. A notice may be posted on a bulletin board or passed by word of mouth. The theory for the company is that this method is cheaper, it utilizes people already in the company, and someone coming in this way (e.g., introduced by a present employee) will be more reliable than an outsider.
2. *The grapevine.* One person tells another at a social or other occasion that a certain department in the company has an opening or will have, and word gets passed along until it reaches someone who is available and interested.
3. *Cold calls.* Résumés and letters are sent to prospective companies by smart job-hunters who don't wait for the Sunday papers or line up at the employment agencies with everyone else in the job market.

Unlocking the Hidden Job Market

Of all the ways to find a job, cold calls take the most time, effort and expense, but are the most successful and usually result in better jobs. They should not, however, be used as a substitute for other methods of finding a job—answering ads, using agencies and other standard sources, but right along with them.

Simply stated, the fastest way to get into the hidden job market is through the mailbox on your corner. For the price of a first-class stamp and an envelope, the U.S. Postal Service will act as your personal messenger and deliver your letter to a selected individual at a company.

The three essential elements for a successful direct mail campaign are:

1. The right mailing list
2. A well-written résumé
3. A good cover letter

Of these (and all three are essential if the effort is to have the best chance of success), the right mailing list is the most important.

Almost every business establishment, from very small local operations to giant multinational corporations, is listed in one or more of the hundreds of directories published each year. These directories do not just list the names and addresses of these companies, they usually include a lot more—frequently names and titles of executives and department managers, product lines, plant locations, sales volume, subsidiaries and financial data.

Some of the more general directories are listed on page 124. They are available at most public libraries. If you want the luxury of having your own directories you can generally purchase them directly from the publishers. They vary in price from fifty to several hundred dollars.

If you want to learn more about a publicly held company, a good source of information is the company's annual report. It is available at no charge by writing to the company, or can be obtained from any stockbroker. Your college placement office may also have them, left by campus recruiters on their perennial visits. Larger public libraries generally have business and economic divisions that keep files of them.

Complete financial information about a publicly held company can also be obtained from their Form 10-K, which must be filed with the Securities Exchange Commission. Copies of these forms will be sent on request by writing directly to the company.

USE DIRECTORIES

Wherever you decide to do research, be prepared to spend a fair amount of time poring over lists of small print. Before you embark on this program you should already have an idea of the kind of work you want to do, know what size company you are interested in and the product or service it sells.

When you are checking the directories, write down the name, address and telephone number of the person you want to reach in each firm you choose. If marketing is your field, find the marketing manager; if you want finance or accounting, pick out the name of the treasurer, controller or chief accountant, and so on. (*Note:* Before sending the material, it pays to call the company, if they are reasonably local, to check on the current status of the person to whom you are writing. Directories are sometimes out of date and people do move.)

Do not send your résumé to a company without directing it to a particular individual in a specific department. Otherwise it may end up in the personnel department where it will settle nicely into a large file cabinet.

Bypass the Personnel Department

Do not send an unsolicited résumé and cover letter to the personnel manager. The personnel department is often the last to know a job is opening up in a company, and if they don't have a specific job order from a department, they will relegate your résumé to the filing cabinet. This is especially true of résumés of applicants seeking entry-level positions.

If you can't obtain a directory or if the directory you have does not list the name of the department manager, telephone the firm. Tell the operator that you want to send some information to the controller, advertising manager, purchasing agent, marketing manager or whatever department head you want to reach, and request the person's name. Most operators, if you sound confident and official, will give you the name or transfer your call to the department where you can make the same request. But don't ask an operator for four or five different department heads and titles—that's a sure tip-off.

Do not tell the operator or a secretary that you are looking for a job or that you are a student. You will immediately be transferred to personnel where you will be told to write a letter and send a résumé. This will result in absolutely nothing, except another 20 cents for the post office and some anxiety for you.

Here's a money-saving tip. Both the telephone company and private firms publish a national "800 directory" which lists every firm that has been assigned an 800 number, giving the caller a toll-free number to call. The telephone company's directory isn't for sale, but an 800 operator will give you any listings you ask for.

When you have extracted from the directories all those lucky companies who are about to be given the golden opportunity to consider you for a position, you are ready to unleash your campaign.

You do this by composing a cover letter, which you enclose when you send a copy of your résumé. This is more than just a simple letter of transmittal. It is not enough to say you are enclosing a résumé and would like to have an interview. Remember, you are not responding to an advertised job. Your experience is limited and you have no idea whether or not a job even exists within the company. Your objective is to convince someone that it would be to his or her advantage to consider you for a position either now or in the future.

Make Your Cover Letter Look Good

Before getting to the contents of your letter, here are some tips on its physical appearance. It must be typewritten; hand-written letters are taboo. If you can't type or don't have a typewriter, find someone who can or does, or hire the services of a public stenographer. A letter must be error free—no strikeovers, no erasures, no misspellings. It must contain your name, address and telephone number. It should also conform to the general standards of a business letter. If you are not familiar with the form, consult a secretary or look it up in a business letter book.

There are three basic elements to a good cover letter.

1. *Attention.* The opening paragraph should be strong enough to immediately make the reader sit up and take notice, but not strong enough to make him wince.
2. *Interest.* The second paragraph should appeal to the reader's self-interest. What can you do for him?
3. *Action.* Suggest a response to your letter.

Here is an example. It can be revised to meet your individual background and requirements.

Dear Mr. Jones:

   I am a copywriter waiting to be discovered, and have been told by my college instructors and certain biased relatives that I do have some talent.

   Since your agency is recognized as one of the leaders in the advertising and marketing of a wide variety of consumer products, I would like very much to be considered for a junior position with your organization. As you can see by the enclosed résumé, I majored in marketing and advertising and was in the top 10 percent of my graduating class.

   I would therefore appreciate an interview where I can present my credentials in person. If there is no opening at this time, perhaps you would be kind enough to offer some advice on how to break into the field of advertising.

   I hope to have the pleasure of hearing from you soon.

   Yours very truly,

   Sagacious T. Finnerty

Other samples of cover letters can be found on pages 57–62.

Much has been written about the effectiveness of mail received on Mondays and Fridays. The consensus seems to be that mail received on those days does not always get read promptly since Monday's mail is heavier than other days, and on Fridays preparation for the weekend interferes with serious work. Perhaps this theory works for mail-order companies, but for job hunting assume that mail is read the day it is received.

Send it out as soon as you have sealed the envelope. Just be sure to say a short prayer to whichever saints (or sinners) govern the creaky machinery of the Postal Service. If the firm is local, consider dropping it off.

Keep a carbon copy of your cover letters and be sure to enter the information on your résumé referral form (see page 12). It is to be hoped that each letter you send out will bring a reply. It's a good idea to attach the replies to your carbon copy. Don't forget to make notes on your index control cards about telephone calls and other facts. These will eventually build up a file based on the initial letter.

Don't be surprised if you don't get invitations to interviews on your first mailing. As a matter of fact, don't be disappointed if you don't even get the courtesy of an acknowledgment. Many people are either too busy, or too lazy, to respond to each letter of application. Good public relations and common courtesy dictate that all correspondence be acknowledged, but it's not done too often.

Obviously, the more correspondence you send out, the better your chances of getting positive results. You *could* get lucky on one or two letters but the odds are against it. You will probably have to send your letter and résumé to at least twenty-five companies before you see tangible results.

No. . .Maybe. . .Yes

Replies will fall into three categories. The first is a polite "Thank you for writing us. There is nothing open now. We will keep your résumé in our files for future reference." In other words, don't call us, we'll call you.

The second standard reply will say that "Nothing is open at our company now. However, if you will complete the enclosed simple application form and return it to our personnel office, we will be glad to keep you on file."

The third, and this is the one you are waiting for, is a reply or a telephone call telling you to come in to discuss a possible position. You will get a lot more of the first and second kinds of replies, but don't discard these. Some can be followed up and turned into interviews.

About two weeks after sending your letter, follow it up with a call. Frequently, the best time is early in the morning, not later than 8 o'clock, before the office staff comes in. Executives get in early (that's how they became executives), and once their secretaries open their desks for business, the protective screen is up and you'll have a tougher time getting through.

When your target gets on the line, be businesslike and pleasant. Don't start the conversation with an apology, but come right to the point. For example:

"Mr. Smith, my name is Mary Keating. I sent you a letter and a résumé on May 22nd. I hope you have had a chance to look at it."

His reply will probably be noncommittal because, first, he may not have seen it, since his secretary might have had instructions to divert job application letters from his desk, and second, he may have seen it but, in the daily rush of business, forgotten both it and your name.

In any case, follow this up with: "You may remember that I have a graduate degree from the Columbia School of Journalism and am looking for a position in corporate communications." If you are told there is nothing open at this time, tell him that "I realize there is no job available, but if you can spare a few minutes of your time, I would appreciate any suggestions on breaking into the field." Executives who are asked for advice are usually flattered and if you're lucky, could be flattered enough to invite you in for a chat, even though there is no job available now. It is an excellent way to make contacts and right now you need contacts more than anything else. The person you speak to is a vital link in a chain. There may be someone he or she knows who knows someone who knows, etc. Also, you may get some good inside information (including trade gossip) that will help you find the job you want. Remember, it's a good idea to have a copy of your résumé and the letter you sent by your side for quick reference.

If you cannot reach the person you want by telephone, send a follow-up letter. It should outline the highlights of your background, and should read something like this:

> Dear Mr. Ramsey:
> On September 19th, I applied for a position with your company and sent you a copy of my résumé.
> You may recall I graduated from Northwestern University with a degree in marketing, and I have had some experience doing market research for the Reynolds Tobacco Company. As a new job-hunter, I would appreciate the opportunity of spending a few minutes with you or a member of your staff to get some advice on finding a position in the marketing field.
> If this is not possible, I am enclosing another copy of my résumé and would appreciate you keeping it in your active file for possible future openings.
> Thank you for your interest and consideration.
> Yours truly,

You would be surprised at how effective a follow-up letter or telephone call can be. Many successful contacts have been make with a little persistence.

Contacts Through the Media

An excellent and productive source of contacts can be found in business and financial magazines, trade journals and your local newspaper, all of which you should be reading while looking for a job. You need not subscribe to them, and those you can't find at your newsstand can be located at your public library. To find the appropriate trade journal, ask the librarian for a copy of the business magazine section of the *Standard Rate and Data Service*. This directory lists all of the trade journals in almost every type of business. When you locate the periodical that covers your particular field, your librarian will probably have the current issue on file. If not, write to the publisher for a sample copy.

Business News Can Be Valuable

Almost every newspaper and business magazine carries news of new enterprises, new firms coming into town, personnel changes and promotions, and new leases signed by local firms. When an employee is promoted, someone else moves up and a new spot opens up at the lower levels. New leases usually mean expansion and that can mean additional staff.

Write a congratulatory note to a newly promoted executive. Nothing pleases a person more than to have someone notice his or her picture or an announcement in the newspaper. Here is a sample of such a note.

Dear Mr. Edwards:

May I offer my congratulations on your recent promotion to Director of Communications of the Consolidated Supermarket Corporation. I thought you might like to have the enclosed clipping from the *Wall Street Journal*.

As a recent graduate of the University of Missouri School of Journalism, with a degree in communications, I am embarking on my first job hunt.

I have taken the liberty of enclosing a copy of my résumé in the event that an opening may occur in your department in the near future.

Again, my very best wishes.

Very truly yours,

Sounds contrived and corny? Maybe so, but the person who receives a note such as this may feel inclined to thank you for noticing and sending the clipping and may even be willing to discuss your problem with you.

The Job Source Form

Before making contact with companies you choose for job possibilities, list them on the job source form found on page 46. You will then have a permanent record of your contacts, their results and follow-up information.

Summing Up

- Seventy-five percent of all jobs are not advertised.
- Reaching the "hidden" job market is hard work but it pays off.

- The right mailing list is the most important element in reaching this market.
- Use specialized directories to compile your list of prospects.
- To obtain complete financial information on a public corporation, request a copy of its Form 10-K.
- *Do not* make your initial contact with the personnel department.
- Find out the name and title of the executive in charge of the department you want to reach.
- Your cover letter should be written in such a way as to get the reader's attention and interest and elicit a response.
- If you don't receive a reply to your letter within two weeks, follow it up with a telephone call.
- Job contacts can be found in your daily newspaper, trade magazines and financial publications.

THE JOB SOURCE FORM

Use this form for listing potential employers before making contact.
As a running record of your prospecting activities, it will make follow-up more productive.

COMPANY	ADDRESS	CONTACT	SOURCE	ACTION AND COMMENTS

7

Outside Help

There are many sources of help available to you as a job-hunter. Among them are employment agencies, résumé services, career counselors, vocational testing services and state and federal agencies. Many of these services can provide you with expert help and advice either at no charge or at moderate cost. There are, however, other services whose main purpose is not to help you but to help themselves at considerable cost to you. It's not always easy to separate the good guys from the bad ones, but a little caution, tempered with some advance information, will help. Here are some typical services of each kind.

Private Employment Agencies

Almost everyone can relate an employment agency horror story—usually heard from someone else. Agencies are accused of being insensitive, unethical, misleading, discourteous and greedy. A few of them are. But think of any other business, profession or service that deals constantly with the general public and you will find the same small percentage who can be similarly accused. And remember, agencies are in business to make money. They don't last long when they alienate their customers.

There are approximately 8000 employment agencies in the United States and each year they place hundreds of thousands of people in jobs in every one of the fifty states and all over the world. Corporations allocate a substantial part of their recruitment budgets to paying agency fees. Employment agencies must be doing something right.

Most of the bad feeling is caused by two considerations: first, looking for a job is a very personal activity. If you are unemployed, your sensitivities increase as you go from one prospect to another, feeling the embarrassment of possible or actual rejection, having to divulge intimate secrets of your background and your goals to complete strangers whose sympathies are not very apparent and whose interest is often neutral at best. So when you go to an employment agency and receive a less than enthusiastic reception, your ego and your pride take a beating. Since the agency is the buffer between you and a job, it becomes the scapegoat for all of your failures and rejections. This is especially true when they don't send you out on a job for which you think you are qualified but they don't.

Second, there is a general lack of understanding as to the orientation of an employment agency. Agencies are *not* in business to find you a job. Their efforts are directed to finding people for employers. Agencies work from job orders supplied by a company and the company expects the agency to expend their effort

47

and time to filling that job order. In other words, agencies' primary concerns—and customers—are companies.

Recognizing this distinction will enable you to make the best possible use of the agency.

WHAT AN AGENCY CANNOT DO FOR YOU

You cannot expect an agency to spend a lot of time to merchandise you to companies. They will try hard to place you with a firm from which they have a suitable job order. But you cannot expect them to provide career counseling except on the most elementary level, such as telling you which bus to get to go to an interview.

You cannot expect an employment agency to prepare your résumé for you unless you are willing to pay them a fee for the service.

You cannot expect an agency counselor to take a personal interest in you or to become upset over the fact that you are unemployed. Most agency counselors work on a commission basis. They get a percentage of the fee when they place you in a position. Human nature being what it is, as an applicant you are either money in the bank or you're not. This leads to quick judgments based on such factors as how you walk, talk and sit. The counselors are pretty good at it, too. While they may lose a good applicant here and there, they have a knack of separating the easy placement from the tough ones. In other words, if you don't fit particular job specifications exactly, they look for someone who does.

On the other hand, there are exceptions. You may be among the fortunate few who may find a counselor who really cares about your problems, who has compassion and who will give you intelligent advice and make a real effort to place you in the right job.

WHAT AN AGENCY CAN DO FOR YOU

Here are some of the reasons why you should use an employment agency.

1. Agencies can save you time by getting you quick interviews.
2. Many job vacancies are listed exclusively with agencies and are not advertised.
3. Agencies can provide you with detailed information about a job and a company that is not available to you through other sources.
4. Many agencies specialize. They concentrate all of their efforts in finding jobs in a particular occupation or profession. Their counselors are chosen for their knowledge of the field and they can be very effective in getting you interviews.
5. Agencies can help you prepare by coaching you on what to say and how to conduct yourself during a particular meeting with a prospective employer.
6. Agency service is usually free to you, and even in those instances where you have to pay a fee, you are under no obligation to pay anything until and unless you accept a position through their efforts.
7. Finally, you should use an agency because you owe it to yourself to exploit every possible source of jobs.

HOW TO CHOOSE AND USE AN AGENCY

Unfortunately, you can't judge an agency until you have used it. However, with a little time and effort you will be able to make an intelligent decision.

The National Association of Personnel Consultants (NAPC) publishes a membership directory, *Access*. This can be obtained by writing to them at 1012 14th Street N.W., Washington, DC 20005. There is a slight charge, but the directory is worth having.

Members of the NAPC have agreed to abide by a code of ethics in working with employers and job applicants. The organization has set standards and testing procedures for their members. Those who pass the qualifying examinations are designated Certified Employment Counselors and use the initials C.E.C. after their names. This doesn't qualify them for immediate sainthood any more than Ph.D., C.P.A., M.D. or J.D. does, but at least it sets some standards. On pages 52–54 you will find a directory of state chapters of the NAPC. They will be happy to answer questions about members in your area.

There are also many good agencies who are not members of NAPC. If you're not sure about a local agency, check with anyone you know who might have used it or the local Better Business Bureau. To find an agency that specializes in your field, look at the classified pages in your local newspaper. Over a period of time you will notice that certain agencies tend to list jobs in certain categories. Concentrate on these first. They are the ones that can most likely help you.

Another way to get the names of good employment agencies is to call the personnel manager of a few of the larger firms in your area. Ask if they would recommend an agency to you. They will probably give you the name of the agency they work with best. Then call that agency and tell them that they were recommended by that company. The agency probably will stand at attention and salute in deference to a recommendation from a good customer.

Agencies have to deal with a large number of applicants and they have to work fast. Because counselors' incomes depend on how many placements they make, the amount of time you will be allotted is minimal. Because you represent little more than an application and a résumé to them, you should check back with them at least once a week by phone or in person. Don't be afraid to remind your counselor that you are still available.

MAKE AN APPOINTMENT

Avoid walking into an agency without an appointment. If you do, you will probably be given an application form to fill out and, after a wait, be directed to the first counselor not on a coffee break.

It's best to call the agency first. If you are answering an ad, describe it on the telephone. Request an appointment or at least get the name of the individual counselor having that particular job. You may be told to mail a résumé. Don't do it. Deliver your résumé personally.

Never go to an employment agency without a résumé. It's your ticket of admission. Leave two copies with the counselor. Although a good counselor may be able to refer you to a job without first having to submit a résumé, many company personnel people are so résumé-oriented that they won't see their mothers without one.

Although most employment agency fees are paid by companies, be sure you ask who pays the bill when being referred to a job. Most agencies will ask you to sign a contract when you first register. Do not sign it until you fully understand the terms—who pays the fee, under what circumstances, how much, how it is to be paid, and guarantee and refund provisions. Ask questions. If you feel you're not getting the right answers, walk out. After you sign the contract, request a copy for yourself.

USE AN AGENCY EARLY

Many job-hunters exhaust other sources before trying an agency. This is a mistake. You may feel that by diligently writing letters, answering ads and pounding the sidewalks, you will get your job without the help of an agency. You could be right. But when you consider that an agency works on your behalf without charge, it doesn't make sense not to use it.

The Public Employment Service

The biggest operator of employment agencies is the federal government. The U.S. Employment Service (USES), a division of the Department of Labor, operates offices in conjunction with the state employment services in virtually every city in the fifty states and Puerto Rico. Their services are free.

What can the state employment service do for you as a new job-hunter? If you are a college graduate, they can do very little. They are more successful in filling unskilled and semiskilled jobs, but not many companies call on their services to fill more substantial positions. The U.S. Employment Service does, however, provide vocational testing programs at no cost. If you are interested in this aspect, check it out with your local office.

Veterans of the armed forces receive special treatment by the USES by law. Disabled veterans are entitled to preferential services.

If you are collecting unemployment insurance benefits, and you want to continue to do so, you are required to use their job referral service whether you like it or not.

Career Counseling Services

Almost every metropolitan newspaper carries advertising offering a variety of jobs and career services. The ads are enticing, promising expert advice on how to get high-paying positions in glamour industries. These services have a few things in common.

1. They do not find you a job (although their advertising intimates they will).
2. They charge substantial fees—from several hundred to several thousand dollars.
3. There are no guarantees or refunds. Once you sign a contract, you're stuck with the entire fee or a major portion of it.

Of course, not every service is a ripoff. Some of these firms are competent, employ qualified, professional counselors, make a serious effort to help you and charge reasonable fees for their work.

How do you know which to choose? One way is to check with the local office of the Better Business Bureau. If their files show more than one or two complaints, keep away. Your local Consumer Protection Agency is also a good source for checking. If you do decide to use one of these services, be sure you do not sign any contract before you fully understand the rights and obligations of the company and yourself. Ask for a copy of the contract to take home and study. If you know a lawyer, have him or her look at it. Be certain you fully comprehend what they are promising for your money. In your eagerness to get a job, it is easy to see and hear only what you want to see and hear. If the contract seems ambiguous, or if you are told one thing but are asked to sign an agreement containing a different set of facts, do not do business with the company.

Résumé-Writing Services

The writing and production of résumés is big business. For a fee of anywhere from $75 to $500 or more, an individual, résumé service, printer or copy service will offer you "expert-professional" résumé writing. For those with lots of experience and a substantial job performance record, it could help. As a new job-hunter, you don't need it.

As a matter of fact, companies can recognize résumés written by commercial résumé services because they are so much alike in style, content and format.

A résumé should be written by the job applicant, and most employers agree that it should be an example of his or her own creativeness and ability and not the product of a standardized résumé service.

Summing Up

- Use employment agencies. They are a good source of jobs.
- Understanding the function of an employment agency will help you work better with it.
- Agencies can get you immediate interviews, sometimes on the same day you register with them.
- Find the employment agencies that specialize and have contacts in your field.
- Most employment agencies do not charge applicants a fee.
- To locate a good agency, call some companies and ask which ones they do business with.
- Avoid walking into an agency without making a prior appointment.
- Use an agency early in your job search.
- Avoid using commercial career counseling services.
- Do not go to a commercial résumé service to prepare your résumé.

NATIONAL ASSOCIATION OF PERSONNEL CONSULTANTS STATE ASSOCIATIONS*

ALABAMA EMPLOYMENT COMMISSION
George Barnes, CPC
Snelling and Snelling
1217 N. Memorial Parkway
Huntsville, AL 35801

ARIZONA ASSOCIATION OF PERSONNEL CONSULTANTS (AAPC)
Mitchell Young
Mitchell Young & Associates
2450 S. 4th Avenue, #305
Yuma, AZ 85364

ARKANSAS PRIVATE EMPLOYMENT AGENCY ASSOCIATION (APEAA)
Devone Payne, CPC
Snelling and Snelling
1049 First National Bank Bldg.
Little Rock, AR 72201

CALIFORNIA ASSOCIATION OF PERSONNEL CONSULTANTS (CAPC)
Glenn English, CPC
Glenn English Agency
7840 Mission Center Ct., #108
San Diego, CA 92108

COLORADO ASSOCIATION OF PERSONNEL SERVICES (CAPS)
Joe Sweeney, CPC
Sweeney Consultants
6825 E. Tennessee, #407
Denver, CO 80222

CONNECTICUT CHAPTER/ NATIONAL ASSOCIATION OF PERSONNEL CONSULTANTS (CC/NAPC)
Louis M. Hipp III, CPC
Hipp Waters Associates
64 Greenwich Ave.
Greenwich, CT 06830

CAPITAL AREA PERSONNEL SERVICES ASSOCIATION (CAPSA-DC)
Frank Grammatica
Ogilvie Associates
7777 Leesburg Pike
Falls Church, VA 22043

PERSONNEL SERVICES ASSOCIATION OF DELAWARE (PSAD)
Abraham Bailis, CPA
Robert Half of Wilmington
Brundywood Plaza
Foulk & Grubb Rds.
Wilmington, DE 19810

FLORIDA ASSOCIATION OF PERSONNEL CONSULTANTS (FAPC)
Ace Kinney
Action Personnel
PO Box 20904
Orlando, FL 32814

GEORGIA ASSOCIATION OF PERSONNEL CONSULTANTS (GAPC)
Betty Arnold, CPC
Arnold Personnel Services, Inc.
150 Interstate North, #220
Atlanta, GA 30339

HAWAII ASSOCIATION OF PERSONNEL CONSULTANTS
Harold Yokoyama, CPC
Associated Services Ltd.
1164 Bishop Street, #407
Honolulu, HI 96813

ILLINOIS ASSOCIATION OF PERSONNEL CONSULTANTS (IAPC)
Hellen Dawson
Employment Professionals Inc.
5005 Newport Drive, #104
Rolling Meadows, IL 60008

---

*Reprinted from *Access* with permission of the National Association of Personnel Consultants.

INDIANA ASSOCIATION OF PERSONNEL CONSULTANTS (IAPC)
Barbara Campbell, CPC
Sunshine Employment
7725 Broadway
Merrillville, IN 46410

IOWA ASSOCIATION OF PERSONNEL CONSULTANTS (IAPC)
Mary Liggett, CPC
M. A. Liggett, Inc.
PO Box 1024
3625 Utica Ridge Rd., #202
Bennendorf, IA 52722

KENTUCKY ASSOCIATION OF PRIVATE EMPLOYMENT SERVICES (KAPES)
Thadd Mudd, CPC
Progress Personnel
1941 Bishop Lane, #202
Watterson City West
Louisville, KY 40218

LOUISIANA ASSOCIATION OF PERSONNEL CONSULTANTS (LAPC)
D. Cleveland Franklin, CPC
Management Recruiters
PO Box 14932
Baton Rouge, LA 70898

MASSACHUSETTS CHAPTER/ NATIONAL ASSOCIATION OF PERSONNEL CONSULTANTS (MC/NAPC)
Blanche Cohen, CPC
Circle Employment Consultants
60 State Street, #3140
Boston, MA 02109

MICHIGAN ASSOCIATION OF PERSONNEL CONSULTANTS (MAPC)
Fred Hertz
Professional Personnel
Consultants
19189 W. Ten Mile Road
Southfield, MI 48075

MINNESOTA ASSOCIATION OF PERSONNEL CONSULTANTS (MAPC)
Mark Sathe, CPC
Sathe & Associates
5050 Excelsior Blvd.
Minneapolis, MN 55416

MISSISSIPPI ASSOCIATION OF PERSONNEL CONSULTANTS (MAPC)
Eddie Frith
Jackson Employment Service
633 N. State Street, #202
Jackson, MS 39202

MISSOURI ASSOCIATION OF PERSONNEL CONSULTANTS (MAPC)
Allen M. Oldfield, CPC
Professional Career Development
7777 Bonhomme, Suite 1326
Clayton, MO 63105

MONTANA ASSOCIATION OF PERSONNEL CONSULTANTS (MAPC)
Roger Koopman
Career Concepts—Bozeman
2304 West Main, #8
Bozeman, MT 58715

NEBRASKA PLACEMENT SERVICE ASSOCIATION (NPSA)
John Naylor
Overland Wolf Center
6910 Pacific Street, #105
Omaha, NE 68106

NEW HAMPSHIRE PRIVATE EMPLOYMENT ASSOCIATION (NHPEA)
Ralph H. Robins
Career Specialists of New England
Box 1084
Portsmouth, NH 03102

NEW JERSEY ASSOCIATION OF PERSONNEL CONSULTANTS (NJAPC)
Jeffrey J. Ryan, CPC
Q Associates
369 Passaic Avenue
Fairfield, NJ 07006

ASSOCIATION OF PERSONNEL CONSULTANTS OF NEW YORK (APCNY)
Carl F. Denny, CPC
Carlden Personnel Services
10740 Queens Boulevard
New York, NY 11375

NORTH CAROLINA ASSOCIATION OF PERSONNEL CONSULTANTS (NCAPC)
Debbie Darr, CPC
Executive Resources
101 S. Marshall Street
Winston-Salem, NC 27101

OHIO ASSOCIATION OF PERSONNEL CONSULTANTS (OAPC)
James Sasse, CPC
James Sasse and Associates
6904 Spring Valley Drive
Holland, OH 43528

OKLAHOMA ASSOCIATION OF PRIVATE EMPLOYMENT SERVICE (OAPES)
Margaret Wick
Wick International
7030 South Yale, #410
Tulsa, OK 74177

OREGON ASSOCIATION OF PERSONNEL CONSULTANTS (OAPC)
Brent Norman, CPC
Murphy, Symonds & Stowell
1001 SW Fifth Avenue, #1110
Portland, OR 97204

PENNSYLVANIA ASSOCIATION OF PERSONNEL CONSULTANTS (PAPC)
Sam Burns
McFadden Associates
1420 Locust Street
Academy House, #210
Philadelphia, PA 19102

RHODE ISLAND CHAPTER/ NATIONAL ASSOCIATION OF PERSONNEL CONSULTANTS (RIC/NAPC)
Anthony Silveira, CPC
Ritta Personnel System
1 Weybosset Hill
Providence, RI 02902

SOUTH CAROLINA ASSOCIATION OF PERSONNEL SERVICES (SCAPS)
Thelma Bridgeman
Atlas Personnel

465 East Kennedy
Spartanburg, SC 29302

TENNESSEE ASSOCIATION OF PERSONNEL CONSULTANTS (TAPC)
William Rasmussen
Rasmussen Associates
904 Executive Park Dr., #130
Knoxville, TN 37919

TEXAS ASSOCIATION OF PERSONNEL CONSULTANTS
Ollie D. Sumrall, CPC
Sumrall Personnel Consultants
4104 McEwen, #450
Dallas, TX 75234

UTAH ASSOCIATION OF EMPLOYMENT AGENCIES (UAEA)
Dave Goodwill
Creative Employment Service
336 South 300 East
Salt Lake City, UT 84111

VIRGINIA ASSOCIATION OF PERSONNEL SERVICES
Verna Falwell
Houston Personnel
2015 Wards Road
Lynchburg, VA 24502

WASHINGTON ASSOCIATION OF PERSONNEL SERVICES (WAPS)
Gary Maybee
Theresa Snow Recruiters
400 108th Ave., NE., #108
Bellevue, WA 98004

WEST VIRGINIA PRIVATE EMPLOYMENT SERVICE ASSOCIATION (WVPESA)
James P. West, CPC
Snelling and Snelling
1007½ Market Plaza
Wheeling, WV 26003

WISCONSIN ASSOCIATION OF PERSONNEL CONSULTANTS (WAPC)
Allan Bley
Placements of Racine, Inc.
425 Main Street, #405
Racine, WI 53403

8

How To Write Letters That Make Friends, Influence People and Get Jobs

Before you successfully complete your job search you will probably become an experienced correspondent. Most contacts you make will require a letter of some kind. Even where you gain an interview through the telephone, it will be necessary for you to write a letter somewhere along the line. There will be replies to advertisements, unsolicited letters to companies, letters to employment agencies, friends, school placement offices and others.

There will be follow-up letters, thank-you letters and acceptance letters. Some of you lucky ones will achieve early success without having to write a single note or letter; for instance, if your father takes a liking to you and offers you a job in his company or your spouse agrees to become the sole breadwinner in the family. The rest of you not so blessed will probably have to write lots of letters.

Résumé Cover Letters

An effective cover letter is more than a simple letter of transmittal. It requires thought and skill to compose one that will get you interviews. It is not enough, for example, to attach a note to your résumé saying, "In reply to your advertisement for an accountant, I am enclosing my résumé," and end with "I hope to hear from you." You might as well just send the résumé without any cover letter at all.

An effective letter should contain the following.

1. Your name and address and a telephone number where you can be reached during the day. If you expect to be out, hire a service or get someone who can be depended upon to take messages.
2. If sent to a box number, the complete address as shown in the ad.
3. If sent to a company, be sure to include the name and the title of the person to whom it is directed, plus the complete name and address of the company.
4. Salutation: Dear Mr. or Dear Ms. (Miss or Mrs. are outdated.) If there is no individual's name in an ad, use "Dear

55

Advertiser." Dear Sir or Dear Madam, Gentlemen, Dear Persons, or Gentlepeople are awkward and outmoded.

5. Call attention to those items in your résumé that relate to qualifications specified in the ad. For example, if the ad calls for a knowledge of electronic data processing and you took some courses in computers, refer to those courses in your letter. If the ad calls for heavy travel and you have no family commitments and feel that you would enjoy traveling, make a definite statement to that effect. Since it's not practical to tailor a different résumé to fit each job, one of the main purposes of the cover letter is to personalize your response.

6. Request for action: Ask for an interview. Don't use "soft" words and sentences such as "I hope I may receive favorable consideration" or "Your consideration would be appreciated." Better to say, "I am available for an immediate interview," or "I would like to present my qualifications in person."

Make no reference to salary desired, even if an advertisement requests it. Salary is a topic that should be discussed in person and never before a first interview.

Neatness Counts

Keep the letter short, three concise paragraphs at most. Don't repeat portions of your résumé, just refer to the pertinent parts of it. Keep it on one page.

Like your résumé, letters should be typed perfectly without errors in spelling or punctuation. The ideal format for a cover letter is a monarch size 7″ × 10″ piece of light-colored stationery with your name and address printed at the top. Of course, each letter must be personally signed. Staple the letter to the résumé so that it does not become separated, and use a standard size business envelope. Never stuff your résumé into a small envelope. It will come out looking like wrapping paper in a fish store.

Although the cover letter is the most important one you will have to write, there are many others that may be necessary during your job search. By using the examples on pages 57–62 as a guide, you should be able to write letters to fit your specific needs.

Summing Up

- A well-written cover letter is as important as your résumé.
- Get the name and title of the addressee. Check spelling if you are not sure.
- Your letter should always contain a phone number where a message can be left at all times.
- Use your letter to refer to specific parts of your résumé that relate to the job you are after.
- Ask for an interview in your cover letter or letter of application.
- Do not discuss salary in a letter. Wait for the interview.
- Keep the letter short and to the point.

Sample Cover Letters

(314) 555-2424

Carol Nelson
13 King Street
St. Louis, MO 63103

August 30, 1983

Ms. Jane Richstone
Midwest Search Associates, Inc.
1325 Borum Street
St. Louis, MO 63153

Dear Jane:

Thank you for discussing the advertised position, Assistant Buyer, with me last week.

As you requested, I am enclosing a copy of my resume. Although I am particularly anxious to get into the retail field, I would be interested in hearing about any opportunity where I can use my education and skills in a growth position.

I have had some experience in sales and customer relations, and I enjoy working with the public. My salary requirements are flexible at this point. I am seeking an opportunity rather than a specific income.

I am available for immediate interviews and would welcome the opportunity of meeting you personally. I will call you in a few days to arrange an appointment.

Cordially,

Carol Nelson

1326 Clayborne Avenue
Stamford, CT 07503
March 2, 1983

Mr. Jack Francis
Art Director
Robert Brown Associates
516 Fifth Avenue
New York, NY 10036

Dear Mr. Francis:

    I am a recent graduate of the School of
Visual Arts, and am seeking a beginner's position
in the art department of a large advertising agency.

    Although my experience is limited to summer
employment, I have a complete portfolio showing
samples of work that I have done in school plus
a few freelance assignments. This includes layout,
paste-ups and mechanicals, lettering and rendering.

    I would like the opportunity of showing
you my work in the possibility that an opening
may occur in your department.

    A resume of my education and background is
enclosed for your information. Thank you for your
consideration.

                Yours truly,

                Marcia Koenig

JANE RADCLIFFE
1293 North Franklin Street
Los Angeles, CA 90857

September 24, 1983

Box 1825M
Los Angeles Times
Los Angeles, CA 90821

Dear Advertiser:

The enclosed resume is submitted in response
to your advertisement for a Junior Research
Assistant listed in the September 23rd edition of
the LOS ANGELES TIMES.

As you can see by my academic background, my
major subject was mathematics. In addition, I took
several courses in market research and economic
analysis. During the last year in college, I was
employed as a research assistant with a major
insurance company.

Since my background and aptitudes seem to
fit the specifications for your position, I would
appreciate the opportunity of an early interview.

Thank you for your consideration.

Yours truly,

JANE RADCLIFFE

SEYMOUR RESTON
1475 Wyatt Avenue
Jenkintown, PA 19134

April 3, 1983

Mr. Leonard Fowler
President
Sanford Pharmaceutical Corporation
4805 N. Franklin Street
Philadelphia, PA 19043

Dear Mr. Fowler:

In the current issue of Sales and Marketing Magazine, there is an item announcing your firm's move to this city from St. Louis. The article further stated that your sales department would be expanding its staff.

I would very much like to be considered for a junior sales position with your organization. I graduated from Temple University with a B.S. in Marketing in 1981 and I am interested in a sales career in the health care industry.

As a native born Pennsylvanian, I am familiar with this area and have many active contacts which can possibly develop into sales leads.

I am enclosing a resume of my qualifications for your review and would appreciate a personal interview with you in order to discuss my qualifications further.

Very truly yours,

Seymour Reston

Fred Richstone
1146 Berry Road
White Plains, NY 10605

(914) 555-6798

July 2, 1983

Ms. Lorna Friedberg
Marketing Director
Franklin, Parker & Smith, Inc.
425 Third Avenue
New York, NY   10021

Dear Ms. Friedberg:

I have just graduated from Columbia University with a Bachelor of Science degree in Marketing, and I am seeking a suitable entry-level position.

Although my working experience has been limited to miscellaneous summer employment, I have had some experience as a part-time assistant in the marketing department of an insurance company.

In return for an opportunity with your firm, I can offer hard work, enthusiasm and a desire to succeed.

I am enclosing a resume for your consideration and would appreciate the opportunity of a personal interview.

Yours very truly,

Fred Richstone

SELMA KIRSCHNER
426 Walnut Street
Philadelphia, PA 19102
(215) 555-1429

November 19, 1982

Mr. Harold Jackson
Director of Operations
Atlantic Bank & Trust Co.
1425 Walnut Street
Philadelphia, PA 19132

Dear Mr. Jackson:

The 1980s represent a unique challenge to banking and financial institutions, both domestic and multinational. As a result, more and more companies are seeking solutions that involve sound financial planning and management.

I believe that my education and training in financial planning will enable me to make a significant contribution to your organization. As a recent graduate of the University of Pennsylvania with a degree in Finance, I have worked for the past four summers on a part-time basis in a variety of business environments. These experiences have given me the opportunity to use my academic training in the real world of business.

Enclosed is a copy of my resume. If you think my qualifications meet your needs at this time, I would like the opportunity for a personal interview.

Sincerely,

Selma Kirschner

9

The Interview—Winners and Losers

A woman once being interviewed for a job as a customer representative with the telephone company was asked why she wanted to work for them. "Because I understand employees get a discount on their telephone bills." She was very promptly turned down.

A twenty-two-year-old recent college graduate in Chicago walked into an interview with a bank and wanted to know whether they had a secured retirement pension plan.

A candidate for an accounting position in Philadelphia told his interviewer that the reason he left his last job was because his supervisor was a "real jerk."

These incidents are not made up. They really happened, and they happen every day. The difference between a successful interview and a disaster does not always depend upon a candidate's qualifications. It often hinges upon some seemingly trivial action, statement or question by the applicant.

Besides inappropriate behavior or responses, the one element that separates the winners from the losers in an interview is preparation.

Personnel managers and recruiters are constantly surprised at the number of job applicants who wander into interviews and then proceed to self-destruct. Like sleepwalkers, seemingly unaware of where they are or what they're doing, they manage in a short period of time to change from viable job candidates into unacceptable nuisances.

In some cases, applicants do not know the full name of the company or have any idea of what it does. In this way, talented people with great scholastic records and good qualifications drift through interviews with vague objectives, completely unprepared for the give-and-take of a successful interview. Then they wonder why it's taking so long to find a job.

This doesn't mean that you have to spend a semester getting yourself into condition to survive an interview. A personnel office is not a police station and your interviewer is not out to trap you into a confession. Some applicants are so tense they walk in looking for the rack. You were not summoned by the Grand Inquisitor, you were invited because the company needs someone to fill a job, and it is hoping that it will be you.

What follows tells how to prepare yourself for the interview; what you should know about the company; what questions to expect and how to answer them; what types of interviews and interviewers to expect; how to field the tough questions; and what to do after the interview.

Personal Appearance

By this time you should not have to be told how to dress when looking for a job. But in case you haven't thought about it, it may come as a surprise that poor personal appearance is frequently at the head of the list of negative factors that lead to rejection of a job applicant during an interview. Getting rejected because you don't have the qualifications for a position or have less experience than another candidate is discouraging but bearable. These are factors that are not actually your fault. But getting written off because of your appearance *is* your fault and has nothing to do with your resemblance to Brooke Shields or Burt Reynolds. The answer is simple: wear appropriate attire.

You may not get the job in the first five minutes of an interview, but you can surely lose it. First impressions are crucial, if not always fair. People are turned on or off by appearance. With acquaintances and blind dates you get enough time to overcome first impressions, but with the limited time allotted for interviews, you win or lose in the first few minutes, sometimes when you walk in the door. The best rule for appearance is not to try to dress the way you think the company wants you to. This is dangerous and can backfire. Dress the same for a bank or an insurance company as you would for an advertising agency or television studio. Of course, different types of firms have different atmospheres. Walk into the creative department of a hot New York advertising agency and you may see some far-out styles. Wander into the board room of a bank and you will think the whole world is colored gray and pin-striped. When you get your job and start working you can adjust your wardrobe to the style of the other people in the company.

As a general rule, be traditional rather than trendy. Men should wear conservatively cut two- or three-piece suits (save the sport jackets and slacks for the office parties or sports events) and women should be attired in conservative dresses or suits. In no instance should anyone wear the great American uniform, jeans.

Check yourself on personal appearance: hair neatly trimmed and combed? Nails clean? Shoes polished? Are you wearing straight stockings or socks? And, definitely, no heavy colognes or perfumes or elaborate costume jewelry. A single pin or tie-clasp is sufficient.

When you walk into the interviewer's office, your mouth should be empty of everything except your tongue and teeth. Don't chew gum or smoke cigarettes. Don't smoke during the interview, even if your interviewer does. If you can't function without a cigarette, smoke it before the interview and leave it in the waiting room.

Preparation—The Key to Success

If you really want to make a good impression, show your interviewer that you have done your homework. Recruiters are tremendously impressed by applicants who are informed about the company, its products or services—and equally disenchanted with those who are not. You would be surprised at how much information is available about a company, but you have to dig for it. It takes time and effort, but it could mean the difference between an offer and a "Don't call us, we'll call you."

Here is what you should know about a company before going into an interview.

1. What does it do? Does it manufacture or distribute products, or does it sell services? What kind? Are the products or services sold to consumers or other businesses?
2. What is the company's annual gross volume?
3. How many people does it employ?
4. Is it a subsidiary or a division of another firm, or is it a holding company? What are the names of the subsidiary companies and what do they do?
5. What are the names and titles of the top executives and managers?
6. What markets does the firm cover—are they national or international?
7. Is it a publicly owned company?
8. What has been the company's growth pattern over the years?

A list of directories that contain this kind of information will be found on pages 124–125. Information about publicly held corporations may also be found in your college placement office.

Where to Obtain Financial Information

Very detailed information about any publicly owned company (e.g., one whose stock is traded on an exchange) can be obtained by writing to it and asking for its Form 10-K, which it must file with the Securities Exchange Commission each year and which contains many details the annual report omits. A 10-K is free, and the company must send it on request.

Information on smaller firms and privately held companies is not as easy to come by. In these cases, your local Chamber of Commerce or State Industrial Development Agency may be able to help you.

With all of the sources available for information, there is no excuse for anyone to walk into an interview without a good knowledge of the company.

If you are referred to a position through an employment agency, your counselor should be able to give you some information about his client. Counselors are in a position to obtain job specifications and company background in great detail—if they are not too lazy to go after them. But it's up to you to ask them the questions that will get you this information. Don't worry about antagonizing the counselor by being insistent. If you are a placeable applicant, he or she knows on which side the agency's bread is buttered. Tell the counselor that your chances of getting the job are much better if you know as much as possible about it. Ask specific questions. If you can't get all the information you want, do your own research.

Kinds of Interviews

Every interview is different. However, most fall into one of three categories. The first can be called the formal or structured interview. Here the interviewer goes by the book—literally. He or she works from a checklist of prepared questions that are pretty much the same for all applicants. The questions are usually direct, requiring specific answers.

This kind of interview forces you to be very specific in your answers and doesn't offer much opportunity for expansion. Many of the questions are designed to evoke a yes or no answer. Take a reasonable time to answer each one. Avoid replying "yes" or "no" to a particular question if you think it requires explanation. Don't allow yourself to be cut off. If you have a point to make that you feel will help you get the job, make it.

Don't judge the entire company by the standards of a single interviewer. This is his or her personal method of determining your qualifications.

The second type of interview is completely opposite in practice. Here the interviewer seems to have no game plan at all. As a matter of fact, the whole thing takes on the casualness of a conversation rather than an interview. You are not asked many specific questions but you have to carry the ball yourself for a good part of the time with general subjects that may seem to be irrelevant to the job or your qualifications for it. Watch out for this type. You may think that your interviewer is a really friendly character who obviously likes you. As a result you get very expansive, lean back in your chair and express yourself freely. It may be a ploy to get you to talk about yourself or it just may be that your interviewer is not really prepared for the interview or is just plain lazy.

In any case the results can be disastrous—for you. The more freedom you have to speak, and the friendlier the atmosphere, the more chance you have of planting both feet firmly in your mouth.

You may leave such an interview feeling euphoric toward the interviewer and the company for allowing you to speak your mind—until you begin wondering whether you really should have admitted that you passed your final exams by the skin of your teeth, or that you would rather travel for a while before settling down to a job, but that your parents threatened to cut off your allowance. I have heard cases of more serious admissions resulting from such social interviews, such as drug arrests and other juicy morsels, which applicants, warmed by the friendliness of the interviewer, thought were great stories to relate.

Watch out for this kind of interview. If you are invited to discuss any aspect of your past life, your friends or your goals in a general way, try to pin it down a bit. Ask your interviewer in what aspect of the matter he or she is interested. Try to keep the interviewer to questions about the job and your qualifications.

The Stress Interview

The third type of interview is known as the stress interview. It is used mostly in interviewing candidates for executive positions, and fortunately, is used much less frequently now than it was a few years ago. There are still interviewers who use it, so you should be forewarned in case you are one of the unlucky applicants who are subjected to it.

The stress interview is purposely and with malice aforethought designed to test your reactions under pressure, the idea being that if you lose control and can't stand the heat of an interview that you may do the same under the stress of the job—a tenuous theory at best.

Here are some of the techniques. Your interviewer starts out by saying: "Tell me about yourself." This sounds innocuous enough, except that he doesn't utter another word for a half-hour, leaving you to fill the void with your own voice. Or, two or more interviewers throw rapid-fire questions at you, concerning your personal habits, your financial condition, your home and family, your sex life and political opinions. They may also criticize your clothing, your school and your background.

While you are speaking, the interviewer may pick up the telephone and make a personal call or proceed to read a magazine.

There are several ways to handle this kind of interview. You can try to keep your cool and handle it as best you can. You can tell your interviewer that you do not feel the questions are fair nor are they relevant, and request that the interview take on a more reasonable pattern. Or you can calmly tell him what you think of any company that treats job candidates like suspected criminals and, on your way out, advise them to stick their job in their ear. Although once very popular with Gestapo types, the stress interview has lost its appeal, except possibly in the U.S. Marine Corps. Companies discovered that they were not only losing good candidates, but also good will.

Questions and Answers

It's not possible to prepare you for every conceivable question you might be asked at an interview. Nor is it possible to give you answers. However, the following is a list of questions frequently asked. It is doubtful if any recruiter will ask all or even most of these questions, but you would be wise to study them and, with a pad and pencil handy, jot down your answers as you go along. Some suggested replies are provided at the end of the list of questions.

GENERAL

Why do you want to work for our firm?
Why did you choose your college major?
Why do you think you would be successful in this position?
Are you familiar with our organization? What do you know about us?
Why do you think this company should hire you?
Tell me about yourself.

EDUCATION

Do you wish to continue your education while working?
Did you participate in extracurricular activities while at school? Which ones?
Did you work at any summer jobs while you were attending school? Where and what did you do?
What was your class standing in school? What was your average grade in your major subject?
Did you receive any scholarships? How much of your tuition did you earn?

OBJECTIVES

In what kind of position are you interested?
What are your goals? Immediate? Long-term?
What would you like to be doing in twenty years?

FINANCIAL

What salary are you looking for?
How much money would you like to be earning in five years?
What is your financial situation? Do you have any savings?

QUALIFICATIONS

Are you willing to go anywhere for a position or do you have specific geographical preferences? Why?

Have you ever made a speech to an audience?

How would you rate your written and oral skills?

What are your major strengths? Your major weaknesses?

How are you at making decisions?

Are you completely familiar with the specifications on this position? Have you any questions about the duties involved?

What background do you have that makes you think you can handle a job such as this?

PERSONAL

Have you been in the military service?

What was your job and your highest rank?

What are your hobbies?

What sports do you participate in?

Would you consider yourself an introvert or an extrovert?

Do you make friends easily?

Can you mix easily and comfortably with a wide variety of people?

Do you read much? What books or periodicals do you prefer?

The following questions are, in many circumstances, illegal. Handle them carefully.

How old are you? (or, When were you born?)

What does your father do? Does your mother work?

What is your mother's maiden name?

Are you now married? Do you intend to get married?

Do you go to church often?

For whom did you vote in the last election?

To what fraternal or social clubs do you belong?

In what country were your parents born?

Do you have plans to rear children?

Tell me the names of your next of kin.

Do you have any physical disabilities?

Your responses to these questions should contain a careful mixture of honesty and discretion. Let's take a few of them and see how they can be handled.

Why do you want to work for our firm?

You may not really know why you want to work for this particular company. The chief reason you're there is probably because you were asked to come in to an interview. Such a reply, however, would be honest, but hardly what the interviewer wants to hear. If the company is well known, the right answer is: "Because your company is a leader in its field," or, "Your firm has an outstanding reputation."

If you're being interviewed by a relatively small firm that is not generally known to the public, a good answer is: "I prefer working with a firm that I can grow with."

Are you familiar with our organization?

Here is where you can show that you have done your homework. Stick to the facts. Tell your interviewer that you know that the firm had gross sales of $165 million last year and that it has declared a dividend every year since 1965, and that it has opened five branch offices in the last five years. Throw in a quote or two from some financial journal if you can. Be absolutely sure your facts are correct and current. And don't go on too long, or it will appear as if you have memorized their annual report.

Why do you think this company should hire you?

"Because you will find me a hard worker who is anxious to learn and who will do everything I can to do a good job for you."

Do you wish to continue your education?

The answer is "yes" even though you are sick and tired of going to school.

How much money would you like to be earning in five or ten years?

Offering a figure would be meaningless in the light of the unknowns that can enter into a future salary projection. It would be wiser to say something to the effect that you would hope to increase your income as you progress through the firm and assume more responsible duties. This answer doesn't really say anything, but the question is silly to begin with.

What do you expect to be doing twenty years from now?

Repress the urge to inform the interviewer that you would like to be on the deck of your yacht off the Bahamas. The answer is "I hope to have a responsible position in management."

So far as your views on travel, you must be flexible, even though you are not too keen on it. Modern business requires people to move about freely and frequently. You may never be asked to make a single trip for the firm, but a categorical "no" at this stage will hurt your prospects for the job. The same goes for relocation. You can respond to that question by stating that you would rather not relocate at this time but you would be willing to go where the company sends you. Don't commit yourself now and hinder the prospects when the need might never arise.

Your major strengths are those that relate to the qualifications for the job. As for weaknesses, you are not aware of any particular ones that will prevent you from performing your duties efficiently. Keep the conversation positive at all times.

IMPROPER QUESTIONS

It is generally against the law to discriminate against anyone for employment because of age. It is also illegal for an interviewer to ask you your age or your date of birth. As a new job-hunter you will have no "age problem" anyway, so don't get uptight if the interviewer asks your age. Technically he or she shouldn't do it, but at your stage of the game it's no big deal. And there is no harm in your answering it.

Some of the other illegal questions you may be asked, however, are much more serious and your responses should be carefully considered.

For instance, "What does your mother or father do? Are you married, or do you intend to get married? Do you go to church? Did you vote in the last election? For whom? What social clubs do you belong to? Do you plan to have children?"

It's awkward to refuse to answer questions at an interview, especially when everything seems to be going well and you are really interested in the job and the company. You may feel that although the question is harmless, your refusal might turn the interviewer against you.

Only you can decide whether or not you want to answer an improper question—but be careful. What you think may be harmless may cost you the job. In answering questions about your marital status, children, politics, etc., you may be playing into the hands of the interviewer who may use his personal prejudices to get rid of you. If you suspect the motive behind a question or do not want to reply out of principle, merely ask in a pleasant way why he or she wants to know. If you are not satisfied with the answer, say that you would rather not reply since the question doesn't appear to relate to your qualifications for the position. If this eliminates you as a prospect, so be it. You can have the consolation of knowing that your principles have not been compromised.

General Tips for the Interview

1. Open your mouth, speak clearly and don't mumble.
2. Use the interviewer's name often during the session. It's a personal touch that helps keep a friendly atmosphere going.
3. Offer your hand upon coming into the office—whether your interviewer does so first or not. Grasp the hand firmly. Offering a handful of rubber fingers or a limp wrist does not engender confidence.
4. Maintain a pleasant look, smile frequently, but don't set your mouth into a permanent grin, unless you want to look like the Halloween pumpkin.
5. Inject enthusiasm into your speech. Act as if you're really glad to be there (even though you would rather be at the movies). Avoid going on in a singsong voice. Your interviewer probably would rather be at the movies too, so try to keep him or her awake.
6. Treat the outer office staff the same way you would treat your interviewer. The receptionist and secretary might be asked for their opinion of you later.
7. If you are asked to fill out an application form before the interviewer, do it without complaint or comments such as "I have a résumé," or "I would rather speak to Ms. Jones first" or "I don't have time for such nonsense." Fill out the form completely. Don't write "see résumé" as a substitute. Your ability to follow instructions is a part of the interview process. If you detect any questions on the application form that you deem to be too personal, leave it blank and discuss it with your interviewer.
8. Arrange your interviews so that you have plenty of time for each one. As a rule, do not schedule more than two interviews a day, one in the morning and one in the afternoon. You cannot judge whether an interview will take one hour or three. You will have enough

pressure on you without having to worry about the time.

9. Sometime near the end of the interview, you will probably be asked if you have any questions. Restrict your questions to those concerning the job specifications and duties. *Don't ask about vacations, benefits or hours.* You're entitled to know about these things, but the first interview isn't the best time to ask.

10. Don't try to entertain your interviewer. It's permissible to inject a little humor into a conversation when it fits in naturally, but don't be a clown.

11. Keep an open mind in your first interview, and don't judge the entire company by the questions or the attitude of the person interviewing you. He or she may seem to be unsympathetic or even unreasonably rough on you but it's a way of getting at the facts.

12. Don't smoke even if your interviewer does and invites you to join him or her—unless you are being interviewed for a job with a tobacco company.

13. Never criticize a former employer, school instructor or anyone with whom you were associated. It's bad form and puts your interviewer on notice that you might have difficulty getting along with people.

14. When the interview is over, don't linger, or use the last few moments to attempt to flatter the interviewer or the company. It will sound phony. Simply say something like: "If I can provide any further information I hope you will contact me," or "Thank you very much for your time, I hope I will be hearing from you again," then leave. For better or for worse, it's all over.

Summing Up

- Preparation is the most important factor in an interview.
- Learn as much as you can about the company before the interview.
- Get copies of the company's annual report and Form 10-K (SEC report).
- Dress conservatively.
- Don't smoke or chew gum.
- Never criticize a former employer.
- Don't allow yourself to be pressured into answering questions simply "yes" or "no."
- Take time to explain your answers when you think it necessary.
- Restrict your answers or statements to subjects relevant to the job and your qualifications.
- Don't ramble—you may say something you could regret later.
- Be positive in all your statements.

- Don't admit to any weaknesses when discussing your qualifications for the job.
- When asked an improper or illegal question, request an explanation or reason for the question before answering.
- Don't be oversensitive when asked about your personal life.
- Do not ask about benefits at your first interview.

10

After the Interview

After all the letter writing, research and sidewalk pounding, you've finally had your chance to tell someone what he or she is missing by not employing you. What do you do now besides breathe a sigh of relief, mutter a short prayer and head for the nearest bar? The first thing you do immediately is to find somewhere to sit down and make notes—your car, a restaurant, the subway or bus, while the interview is still fresh in your mind.

A great deal of information has passed between you and the interviewer. He or she is busily making notes on you. You owe it to yourself to do the same. Should you be called back for a second interview with another interviewer, many of the same questions may be asked again. It's helpful to be consistent in your answers. The "Interview Review Form" on page 75 can serve as a guide to the types of questions you should ask yourself following each interview.

Writing the "Thank You" Letter

When you get home, transcribe the notes you made onto the index card you are maintaining for each contact. Next, you should sit down and write a letter to the person who interviewed you, thanking him or her for their time. It is so rarely done that its impact is astounding. Recruiters and personnel people spend most of their working time asking the same questions, listening to the same answers and going through the same scenario every day. What may seem to be a special event to you is a tedious chore to them.

When they get a personal note from a thoughtful applicant, they appreciate it, and that applicant is remembered.

The letter should be short and sincere. Do not attempt to restate your case. It should consist of three short thoughts:

1. Thank the recruiter for giving you the opportunity to present your qualifications.
2. Mention the fact that you believe you can do the job as outlined.
3. Express the hope that you will be favorably considered for the position. For example:

Dear Mr. Smith:

Thank you for giving me the opportunity to present my qualifications for the position of Junior Financial Analyst.

I enjoyed the interview and feel certain that given the oppor-

73

tunity, I can efficiently perform the duties of the position as you described them. In addition, I was most impressed with the information you provided about the future of the company and the potential of the position.

Your favorable consideration will be very much appreciated.

Yours truly,

What if you are not sure you want to work for this company? You may have other irons in the fire and anticipate other interviews. Write the letter anyway. You will be making a friend. Also, this may turn out to be the best of all opportunities that come along and if you find a better job you can always turn the job down if it is offered. Examples of other letters are found on pages 57–62.

The final thing to do after the interview is to take a hard look at your performance. Recall what questions were asked and review your responses. Did you make a complete ass of yourself? If you did, admit it and learn from it. Be a harsh critic even if it's painful. If you learn something from each interview, you will do better in the next one. Ask yourself:

1. Did I forget to mention anything that would have helped me? About my education? About my experience?
2. How was my personal appearance? Did I wear the right outfit? Was everything clean and pressed?
3. Was I aggressive enough? Did I come on too strong?
4. Was I too cool? Did I show a lack of interest or enthusiasm?
5. Did I ask the right questions?
6. Do I have all the information I need about the job?
7. Did I talk too much or not enough?
8. Did I make any serious gaffes? Am I overestimating their importance?

Write down all your impressions of the interview and indicate where you think you can improve your techniques so that you can do better in your next interview.

Summing Up

- Immediately after the interview is over, write down everything that transpired while fresh in your memory.
- Write a letter to the interviewer, thanking him or her for their time.
- Carefully review your performance at the interview.
- Write down all of your impressions, good and bad.
- Plan how to improve yourself at your next interview.

Interview Review Form

Use this model to make your own forms. Complete one after every interview. Write your impressions of the company and the interviewer. Note all aspects of the interview including discussions of salary, responsibilities, future prospects— any information that will help you recall the interview when needed. It will help you remember important facts when called in for second interviews and help you in your follow-up.

Company _____

Address _____ Telephone _____

Product or Service _____

Position _____

Salary and benefits _____

Source _____

(Advertisement, direct contact, personal, etc.)

Description of duties and responsibilities _____

_____

_____

Interviewer and title _____

General interview notes _____

_____

_____

_____

_____

_____

_____

Impressions of position and company _____

_____

_____

_____

Conclusions _____

_____

_____

Follow-up _____

11

Women in the Job Market

If you are a woman looking for a job, you've come along at the right time. Not so long ago a woman seeking employment in occupations other than clerk, stenographer or receptionist had a much rougher time than men. Most firms, large and small, were run by men, for men, and practically your only entry into this world was through the typewriter.

Until the 1960s newspaper classified advertising was divided into two sections: Help Wanted—Male and Help Wanted—Female, and the woman who had the temerity to inquire about a job listed in the male column was told in no uncertain terms that she was not wanted. Life was simpler then—for men. All a recruiter had to do when the wrong sex wanted the right job was to smile and say "Sorry, we want a man for this job." And there was nothing anyone could do about it.

The picture is very much different now. That doesn't mean that all doors are open for women in the job market—there is still plenty of resistance around. But the activities of the women's rights movement, and the laws that have been passed as a result of those activities, have made most companies change their ways. It's not a matter of altruism. The courts now say the doors will be open and companies must comply.

If you are a college graduate with an M.B.A., Fortune 500 companies are anxious to bring you into their training programs at unprecedented salaries— now they are almost saying "Men need not apply."

Before this gets too heady, however, you should know that you still have lots of competition in the job market from other women as well as men. But you do have help.

Women's Networks

There is an important word on the job horizon. It is "networking." It's the female version of the "old boy" system which provided professional and social contacts in men's clubs, fraternities, trade and business associations.

Women's groups of all kinds have adopted this networking technique, and almost every city has workshops, symposiums and job clinics for all occupations.

Seminars in self-awareness, career pathing, legal rights and similar subjects are organized to help the transition of women into what was once a male-dominated job market.

There is a list of organizations, periodicals and books of particular interest to career-oriented women at the end of this chapter.

Although many corporations have made a real effort to abide by the spirit and letter of the equal opportunity laws, there is still much discrimination against women. In many cases, it's hard to pin down because it's done very subtly. No company representative in his right mind would blatantly flout the law—it could get the firm and him into a lot of hot water.

What to Watch Out For

Usually, there are a large number of jobs listed in the newspaper under the heading "Administrative Assistant." This is usually a ruse used by companies and employment agencies who are in reality looking for secretaries. Since they are in short supply, and women now want to be more than secretaries, employers hope that by disguising the title of the job they will attract many more applicants. And they do. So, unless you want a job as a secretary, avoid the Administrative Assistant ads.

As a general rule, any ad that requires "good skills" is seeking typing and shorthand. Getting into the door through the use of secretarial skills is still done and should be considered a viable option when the market is tight for your specialty. Many women executives started out by accepting a job as a secretary and worked up through the organization. However, good secretaries usually remain secretaries, and the chances of rising to the top through the typewriter are not that great.

There are exceptions to this rule. If you have your heart set on a creative job in publishing, advertising, public relations, etc., it is difficult to find an employer who will take a chance on unproven talent. Practically the only way to break into these occupations is through the clerical or secretarial desk, and many advertising and publishing executives started out that way. It will certainly do you no harm to learn to operate a typewriter in any case. I would recommend the same to male readers. With computer video terminals and word processing systems now a part of every office, the typewriter keyboard has become a permanent fixture.

Be especially careful in dealing with employment agencies. Because of the demand from their clients for secretarial and clerical help, agencies will try to shunt women into those kinds of jobs. They will promise you that you are entering an executive training program and that your secretarial status will only be temporary. Check the job out carefully!

If you study some of the ads run by employment agencies in your local newspaper, you will see them listed under the titles Executive Assistants or Administrative Assistants. Along with them, in bold type to catch your attention, may be the words: TRAVEL FREE—MEET CELEBRITIES—ART—AIRLINES—WORK WITH PEOPLE—PLUSH OFFICE—PUBLISHING—GLAMOUR JOB and others designed to grab you. Somewhere in the fine print will be the words "good skills," and it will be another secretarial job.

Try to register with professional placement agencies only. The others will be interested in your typing ability and skip the rest of your background and education. If you do contact an agency about an advertised job for which you have the qualifications, and you have the feeling that they are trying to talk you out of it, the chances are they want a man for the job. Gently remind them of the sex discrimination laws. You would be surprised at how quickly they change their tune.

Equal Work—Equal Pay

A word about salaries. The Women's Bureau of the U.S. Department of Labor, in a recent survey, stated that although a little more than one-half of the civilian labor force consists of women, the average salary of those employed full-time is about three-fifths of the salaries for full-time male workers.

The law specifically states that in the matter of pay, there can be no distinction between men and women when the work is equal. How sensitive you allow yourself to be and what you decide to do about an obvious case of wage discrimination is a personal decision. You're after your first job, so be flexible. If you suspect you are being offered a job at a lower salary than they would offer a man, and you're sure of your facts, you can either walk out, file an official complaint or accept the job and do your best to prove to your new employer that you can do the job better than anyone else, male or female, and are entitled to more money.

Summing Up

- More jobs are open for women now than ever before, but there is still discrimination.
- Check the "networking" facilities in your area by contacting professional and business groups.
- Female M.B.A.'s are in demand by top corporations.
- Employers disguise help-wanted ads for secretaries with pretentious titles.
- Be suspicious of "executive training programs" that require typing and shorthand.
- Women are, by law, entitled to the same pay as men if they perform the same work.

Business and Professional Women's Organizations

Advertising Women of New York
153 East 57th Street
New York, NY 10011
    Publication: *Ad Libber*

American Business Women's Association
9100 Ward Parkway
Kansas City, MO 64114
    Publication: *Women in Business*

American Medical Women's Association
465 Grand Street
New York, NY 10001
    Publication: *Monthly Journal*

American Society of Professional and Executive Women
1511 Walnut Street
Philadelphia, PA 19102
>Publications: *Ascend Report*
>*Quarterly Newsletter*

American Society of Women Accountants
35 East Wacker Drive
Chicago, IL 60601
>Publications: *The Coordinator*
>*The Woman CPA*

American Women in Radio and Television*
1321 Connecticut Avenue
Washington, DC 20036
>Publication: *Women on the Job: Careers in Broadcasting*

American News Women's Club
1607 22nd Street, N.W.
Washington, DC 20008
>Publication: *Shop Talk*

Association for Women in Science*
1346 Connecticut Avenue
Washington, DC 20036
>Publications: *Newsletter*
>*Job Bulletin*

Association of Women in Architecture*
7440 University Drive
St. Louis, MO 63130

Catalyst
14 East 60th Street
New York, NY 10022
>Publications: *Self-Guidance Education & Career Booklets*
>*The Catalyst Career Guide For Women*
>*Guide to Successful Résumés & Interviews*

American Society for Public Administration
1255 Connecticut Avenue, N.W.
Washington, DC 20036
>Publications: *Public Administration Review*
>*Public Administration Times*

Financial Women's Association of New York*
1 Bankers Trust Plaza
New York, NY 10006
>Publication: *Monthly Newsletter*

National Association of Bank Women
500 North Michigan Avenue
Chicago, IL 60611

---

*Student Membership Available

National Association of Female Executives*
123 East 54th Street
New York, NY 10022
    Publications: *The Executive Female Magazine*
              More Money Newsletter

National Association of Media Women*
1185 Niskey Lake Road, S.W.
Atlanta, GA 30331
    Publication: *Media Woman*

National Association of Women Artists
41 Union Square
New York, NY 10003
    Publication: *Annual Exhibition Catalog*

National Federation of Business and Professional Women's Clubs*
2012 Massachusetts Avenue, N.W.
Washington, DC 20011
    Publication: *National Business Woman*

National Organization for Women*
425 13th Street
Washington, DC 20004
    Publication: *National NOW Times*

Society of Women Engineers*
345 East 47th Street
New York, NY 10017

Women in Sales Association*
21 Cleveland Street
Valhalla, NY 10595
    Publication: *Sales Leader*

Women in Communications*
P.O. Box 9561
Austin, TX 78766
    Publication: *Careers in Communications*

Magazines for Career-Oriented Women**

ESSENCE
1500 Broadway
New York, NY 10036

For young black women.

GRADUATE WOMAN
2401 Virginia Avenue, N.W.
Washington, DC 20037

Edited for action-oriented women concerned with women's issues, problems, history—by, for and about women.

---

*Student Membership Available
**Reader descriptions from publishers' statements

MS.
119 West 40th Street
New York, NY 10018

Forum for women and men to share information about their changing roles.

NEW WOMAN
P.O. Drawer 189
Palm Beach, FL 33480

Guidance, information and way of life for active women in all walks of life, careers, new styles in marriage.

SAVVY
111 Eighth Avenue
New York, NY 10011

For success-oriented women.

SELF
350 Madison Avenue
New York, NY 10017

Edited for educated, active women of today.

WORKING MOTHER
230 Park Avenue
New York, NY 10017

For working women with children under eighteen years living in the household.

WORKING WOMAN
1180 Avenue of the Americas
New York, NY 10036

For the career woman, with articles on finance, jobs and business.

Books for the Career Woman

Abarnel, Karin and Siegel, Connie M. *Women's Work Book: How to Get Your First Job, How to Re-Enter the Job Market, How to Fight For Your Rights in the Work World, and More.* New York: Warner Books, 1977.

Agassi, Judith B. *Women on the Job: The Attitudes of Women to Their Work.* Lexington, MA.: Lexington Books, 1979.

Bird, Caroline and McKay, David. *Everything A Woman Needs To Know To Get Paid What She's Worth.* New York: Bantam Books, 1981.

Cowan, Susan and Sandman, Peter M. *From College Girl to Working Woman: 201 Big-City Jobs for Girl Graduates.* New York: Macmillan Company, 1970.

Dunlap, Jan. *Personal and Professional Success for Women.* Englewood Cliffs, NJ: Prentice-Hall, 1972.

Higginson, Margaret V., and Quick, Thomas L. *The Ambitious Woman's Guide to a Successful Career.* New York: Amacom, 1980.

Kleiman, Carol. *Women's Networks.* New York: Ballantine, 1981.

Lederer, Muriel. *Blue-Collar Jobs for Women.* New York: E.P. Dutton, 1979.

Malloy, John T. *The Woman's Dress for Success Book.* Reardon & Walsh, 1978.

Mitchell, Joyce Slayton. *I Can Be Anything: Careers and Colleges for Young Women.* New York: Bantam, 1978.

Myers, Henry. *Women At Work.* Princeton, NJ: Dow Jones-Irwin, 1979.

Pinkstaff, Marlene A., and Wilkinson, Anne B. *Women at Work: Overcoming the Obstacles.* Reading, MA: Addison-Wesley Publishing Co., 1979.

Pogrebin, Letty Cottin. *Getting Yours: How To Make the System Work for the Working Woman.* New York: Avon, 1981.

12

Your Legal Rights In The Job Market

It is illegal for an employer or an employment agency to disqualify you for a position for any of the following reasons:

Age
Race
Creed
Color

Religion
National Origin
Sex
Marital Status

Therefore, you can go out there confident in the knowledge that no matter who or what you are, you stand equal in the market place. Right?

Wrong. The Congress, the U.S. Supreme Court, your state legislature and your city council can fill entire libraries with equal rights statutes, but they cannot prevent discrimination any more than they can prevent bank robberies.

This is not to say that all companies flagrantly flout laws. The vast majority of corporations make a sincere effort to uphold the law and set policies to adhere to both the spirit and letter of the law in their hiring practices. This is not altogether altruistic in all cases. Companies who do business with the government and want to continue to do so don't want the problems or publicity of adverse action.

To paraphrase a popular slogan, "Companies don't discriminate, people do," and this is where the trouble lies.

When you are being interviewed for a position, you are on a one-to-one basis with your interviewer, who, as an individual, may consciously or otherwise carry prejudices. Relationships are built to a great extent on the chemistry between two people. It is even more prevalent between an applicant and an interviewer where quick judgments are made.

However, with the best intentions and sincere efforts of a company, there are some people who purposely and maliciously exercise their personal prejudices in hiring, promoting and firing. It is all very subtle and usually unprovable. When these people are eventually found out, the result is usually a costly court case.

Discrimination: *How Can You Tell*?

It's not easy to tell when you are being turned down for a job whether or not you are a victim of discrimination. There are many legitimate reasons why you may not be acceptable. But actually, it all comes down to whether the interviewer likes you. It's a matter of personal chemistry between the people, and if the vibrations are wrong, nothing in your background or education will make up for it. Very few of us can be completely objective in dealing with people.

The point is that if you're not treated in a manner you think is due you or you are turned down when you believe you are the perfect candidate for the job, it doesn't necessarily mean that you are the victim of illegal discrimination.

If, however, you really believe you are being denied a job due to discriminatory practices, don't panic at the interview. Keep your cool. When you get home, review the situation very calmly. And then think it over again the next day. Are you really being discriminated against, and this is the big question, can you substantiate it?

Even if your intuition is strong and you think you have a solid case, do you want to go through the hassle of bringing a formal complaint? It can cost you time and effort, and it certainly won't get you a job.

If you do decide to lodge a complaint against an employer, consult an attorney or contact your local office of the U.S. Equal Employment Opportunity Commission. For further information on laws and your rights, you can write to: Equal Employment Opportunity Commission, 2401 E Street, Washington, DC 20506.

13

Apprenticeship Training

No book on the first-time job hunter would be complete without a reference to the National Apprenticeship Program. Encouraged and helped by the Employment and Training Administration of the U.S. Department of Labor, the program is a cooperative endeavor between management and labor to provide on-the-job training to people eager to learn skills that will insure them of good paying, satisfying jobs in the labor market.

While the majority of training positions that come under the apprenticeship program are "blue collar," many lead to highly skilled technical jobs and responsible supervisory positions.

What Is Apprenticeship?

Apprenticeship is a system of on-the-job-training in many occupations that requires a wide range of both skills and knowledge. It involves planned day-by-day work on the job, under close supervision, combined with academic-type studies in related subjects.

Apprenticeship provides instruction and experience on and off the job in both practical and theoretical aspects of the work involved.

Through rotation from one kind of related task to another and instruction, apprentices acquire skills that enable them to be productive and earn wages while undergoing instruction and training.

Apprenticeship terms range from one to five years, depending upon the occupation involved.

What Can Apprenticeship Offer the New Employee?

Well-planned, properly supervised programs can:

1. Give new and displaced workers the opportunity to develop skills.
2. Assure a supply of skilled people to meet industrial and community needs.
3. Give trained workers greater job security.
4. Develop supervisory and managerial skills.
5. Raise general skill levels.

As a young worker just entering employment, apprenticeship offers you the opportunity to acquire skills to help you to get a job and the chance to earn while you learn. Management and labor cooperate to provide these jobs. The instructors are experienced workers passing on their skills and know-how to newcomers. Management and labor cooperate with government and the educational system at the national, state and local levels.

Apprentices are employed in every major industry—construction, health, manufacturing, service and other fields. Young people considering apprenticeship have the opportunity to choose from among more than 500 occupations.

How to Apply

Information on apprenticeship opportunities and how to apply for them is available from area offices of the apprenticeship information centers and state employment service offices. Applicants can also check with firms that have workers in a trade that interests them, the local unions representing that trade, or the joint apprenticeship committee. School counselors are another source of apprenticeship information.

Programs are often set up by labor unions, women's groups and others to advise applicants on apprenticeship opportunities and help them prepare for entrance examinations. To find the programs in your area, consult the staffs of local or regional offices or state apprenticeship agencies. A partial list of their office locations is at the end of this chapter.

Information is also available from:

Bureau of Apprenticeship and Training
U.S. Department of Labor
601 D Street N.W.
Washington, DC 20213

Occupations that Employ Apprentices

Federal regulations define an apprenticeable occupation as one that:

1. Can be learned through a structured program of supervised on-the-job training;
2. Is clearly identified and commonly recognized throughout an industry;
3. Involves manual, mechanical or technical skills and knowledge that require a minimum of 2000 hours of on-the-job work experience;
4. Requires related instruction to supplement on-the-job training. This instruction may be given in a classroom, through correspondence courses or self-study.

The Bureau of Apprenticeship and Training has approved over 500 occupations as apprenticeable, and new occupations are constantly being added to keep pace with technological advances.

If your career interests lie in the direction of a skilled trade, no matter what your education, you should look into the apprenticeship training program.

Summing Up

- Apprenticeship programs provide on-the-job training and education for people who want to learn a trade.
- It offers young workers just entering employment the chance to learn skills to help get a job and earn while you learn.
- The program is coordinated through the U.S. Department of Labor in cooperation with private industry and labor unions.
- Information about training programs can be obtained through your local office of the Bureau of Apprenticeship and Training.

Bureau of Apprenticeship and Training
State and Area Offices*

Alaska
Room E-551
Federal Bldg. and Courthouse
Box 37
Anchorage 99513

Alabama
1931 Ninth Ave., South
South Twentieth Bldg.
Birmingham 35205

Room 80, JCN Bldg.
200 Sparkman Dr.
Huntsville 35806

Room 418
951 Government St. Bldg.
Mobile 36604

Arizona
1330 North First St.
Phoenix 85004

Room 2-K
301 West Congress St.
Tucson 85701

Arkansas
Room 3014 Federal Bldg.
790 West Capitol St.
Little Rock 72201

California
Room 3235, Federal Bldg.
300 North Los Angeles St.
Los Angeles 90012

Room 215 Post Office Bldg.
P.O. Box 2006
8th and I Sts.
Sacramento 95809

Room 6S-27, Federal Bldg.
880 Front St.
San Diego 92188

Room 344
211 Main St.
San Francisco 94105

Colorado
Room 464, U.S. Custom House
721 19th St.
Denver 80202

Connecticut
Room 301-A. U.S. Courthouse
Federal Bldg.
915 Lafayette Blvd.
Bridgeport 06603

Rooms 236–237, Federal Bldg.
135 High St.
Hartford 06103

Delaware
Room 205
U.S. Post Office Bldg.
11th and Market Sts.
Wilmington 19801

---

*Reprinted from "The National Apprenticeship Program," published by the U.S. Department of Labor, Employment and Training Administration.

Florida
955 NW., 119th St.
Miami 33168

Box 35082
400 West Bar St.
Jacksonville 32202

Suite 264
2574 Seagate Dr.
Tallahassee 32301

Room 605
700 Twiggs St.
Tampa 33602

Georgia
Room 725
1371 Peachtree St.
Atlanta 30309

Room 101
307 15th St.
Columbus 31901

Room 236, Post Office Bldg.
P.O. Box 8121
Savannah 31402

Hawaii
Room 5113
300 Ala Moana Dr.
Honolulu 96850

Idaho
Suite 2
3010 West State St.
Boise 83703

Illinois
Suite 101
3166 Des Plaines Ave.
Des Plaines 60018

Suite 250
707 Berkshire Ave.
East Alton 62024

Rooms 401 and 505
7222 West Cermak Rd.
North Riverside 60545

Room 319
First National Bank Bldg.
228 NW Jefferson Ave.
Peoria 61602

Room 150, Federal Bldg.
211 South Court St.
Rockford 61108

Room 102
U.S. Post Office and Courthouse
600 East Monroe St.
Springfield 62701

Indiana
Room 240, Federal Bldg. and U.S.
Courthouse
101 NW Seventh St.
Evansville 47708

Room 110
343 West Wayne St.
Fort Wayne 46802

Room 108
610 Connecticut
Gary 46401

Room 414, Federal Bldg. and U.S.
Courthouse
#46 Ohio St.
Indianapolis 46204

Room 430, Sherland Bldg.
105 East Jefferson St.
South Bend 46601

Room 313, Post Office Bldg.
30 North Seventh St.
Terre Haute 47808

Iowa
Room 314-B, Federal Bldg.
131 East Fourth St.
Davenport 52801

Room 637, Federal Bldg.
210 Walnut St.
Des Moines 50309

Kansas
Room 225, Federal Bldg.
444 SE Quincy St.
Topeka 66683

Suite 50-LL
O. W. Garvey Bldg.
200 West Douglas
Wichita 67202

Kentucky
Suite 201, 1200 Bldg.
1200 South Broadway
Lexington 40504

Room 187-L, Federal Bldg.
600 Federal Pl.
Louisville 40202

Louisiana
Room 215-B, Hoover Bldg.
8312 Florida Blvd.
Baton Rouge 70806

3731 Ryan St.
P.O. Box 5943
Lake Charles 70601

600 South St.
618 F. Edward Herbert Bldg.
New Orleans 70130

Room 8A-09, Federal Bldg.
500 Fannin St.
Shreveport 71101

Maine
Room 101-B, Federal Bldg.
68 Sewell St.
Augusta 04330

Room 327, Post Office Bldg.
76 Pearl St.
P.O. Box 54
Portland 04112

Maryland
Room 1028, Federal Bldg.
Charles Center
31 Hopkins Plaza
Baltimore 21201

Room 213, Allegany County Office
Bldg.
#3 Pershing St.
Cumberland 21502

129 West Main St.
P.O. Box 366
Salisbury 21801

Massachusetts
Room 1001, JFK Federal Bldg.
Government Center
Boston 02213

Room 801
1200 Main St.
Springfield 01103

Room 500, Federal Bldg.
U.S. Courthouse
Worcester 01601

Michigan
Room 2-1-60
Battle Creek Federal Center
74 North Washington Ave.
Battle Creek 49107

Room 658, Federal Bldg. and U.S.
Courthouse
231 West Lafayette Ave.
Detroit 48226

Room 186, Federal Bldg.
110 Michigan, NW.
Grand Rapids 49502

Rooms 206 and 308, Carr Bldg.
300 East Michigan Ave.
Lansing 48933

Suite 210
Marquette City Hall
220 West Washington St.
Marquette 49855

N. Warren at E. Genesee St.
P.O. Box 1017
Saginaw 48606

Minnesota
Room 204, Federal Bldg.
515 West First St.
Duluth 55802

Room 134, Federal Bldg. and U.S.
Courthouse
316 Roberts St.
St. Paul 55101

Mississippi
Security Markham Bldg.
2300 14th St.
Gulfport 39501

Room 6
5760 I-55 North
Jackson 39211

Missouri
Room 2111, Federal Office Bldg.
911 Walnut St.
Kansas City 64106

Room 547
210 North 12th Blvd.
St. Louis 63101

Montana
Room 1414, Federal Bldg. and U.S.
Courthouse
316 North 26th St.
Billings 59101

Room 394, Drawer #10055
Federal Office Bldg.
301 South Park Ave.
Helena 59601

Nebraska
Room 700
106 South 15th St.
Omaha 68102

Nevada
Room 316, Post Office Bldg.
301 East Stewart Ave.
Las Vegas 89101

Room 310, Post Office Bldg.
P.O. Box 3517
50 South Virginia St.
Reno 89501

New Hampshire
Room 321, Federal Bldg.
55 Pleasant St.
Concord 03301

New Jersey
Room 838, New Federal Bldg.
970 Broad St.
Newark 07102

Room 14
96 Bayard St.
New Brunswick 08901

Room 401, U.S. Post Office and
Courthouse
402 East State St.
Trenton 08608

New Mexico
Room 1116, Western Bank Bldg.
505 Marquette, NW.
Albuquerque 87102

New York
Room 512
U.S. Post Office and Courthouse
Albany 12207

Room 311
15 Henry St.
P.O. Box 308
Binghamton 13902

Room 214, U.S. Courthouse
69 Niagara Sq.
Buffalo 14202

Room LL-1
585 Stewart Ave.
Garden City 11530

Room 506
26 Federal Plaza
New York 10007

Room 607, Federal Bldg. and U.S.
Courthouse
100 State St.
Rochester 14614

Room 1241, Federal Bldg. and U.S.
Courthouse
100 South Clinton St.
Syracuse 13202

North Carolina
Room 415, BSR Bldg.
316 East Morehead St.
Charlotte 28202

Room 376, Federal Bldg.
Raleigh 27601

North Dakota
Room 344, New Federal Bldg.
653 Second Ave., North
Fargo 58102

Ohio
Room 208, Federal Bldg.
201 Cleveland Ave., SW.
Canton 44702

Room 2112, Federal Office Bldg.
550 Main St.
Cincinnati 45202

Room 720, Plaza 9 Bldg.
55 Erieview Plaza
Cleveland 44114

Rooms 605 and 407
200 North High St.
Columbus 43215

Room 312, Federal Bldg. and U.S.
Courthouse
118 West Third St.
Dayton 45404

Room 7206, Federal Office Bldg.
234 Summit St.
Toledo 43604

Room 311, U.S. Post Office Bldg.
9 West Front St.
Youngstown 44501

Oklahoma
Suite 1440
50 Penn Pl.
Oklahoma City 73118

Suite 308
Center Mall Professional Bldg.
717 South Houston Ave.
Tulsa 74127

Oregon
Room 231, Federal Bldg.
211 East Seventh
Eugene 97401

Room 835
1220 SW Third Ave.
Portland 97204

Pennsylvania
2nd Floor
615 Howard Ave.
Altoona 16601

Room 106, Federal Bldg.
6th and State St.
Erie 16507

Rooms 770 and 773
Federal Bldg.
228 Walnut St.
Harrisburg 17108

Room 4252, Wm. J. Green, Jr.
Federal Bldg.
600 Arch St.
Philadelphia 19106

Room 1102, Federal Bldg.
1000 Liberty Ave.
Pittsburgh 15222

Room 2115
East Shire Office Bldg.
45 South Front St.
Reading 19603

Room 2028
20 North Pennsylvania Ave.
Wilkes-Barre 18701

Rhode Island
Federal Bldg.
100 Hartford Ave.
Providence 02909

South Carolina
Room 231, Federal Bldg.
344 Meeting St.
Charleston 29403

Suite 201-B, Federal Bldg.
901 Sumter St.
Columbia 29201

South Dakota
Room 104, Federal Bldg.
400 St. Phillips Ave.
Sioux Falls 51102

Tennessee
Suite 7003, 6300 Bldg.
Eastgate Center
Chattanooga 37411

Room 232
301 Cumberland Ave.
Knoxville 37902

Room 209, Federal Office Bldg.
167 North Main St.
Memphis 38103

Suite 406
1720 West End Ave.
Nashville 37203

Texas
Room 578, Federal Office Bldg.
300 East Eighth St.
Austin 78701

Room 324, Federal Bldg.
300 Willow St.
Beaumont 77701

Room 425, United Savings Bldg.
3765 South Alameda
Corpus Christi 78411

Suite 503
1499 Regal Row
Dallas 75247

Room #1
1515 Airway Blvd.
El Paso 79925

Room 9A08, Federal Bldg.
819 Taylor St.
Fort Worth 76102

Room 2102, VA Bldg.
2320 La Branch St.
Houston 77004

Room 416-1, Federal Bldg.
1205 Texas Ave.
Lubbock 79401

Room B-414, Federal Bldg.
727 East Durango
San Antonio 78206

Utah
Room 314, Post Office Bldg.
350 South Main St.
Salt Lake City 84101

Vermont
Suite 103, Burlington Sq.
96 College St.
Burlington 05401

Virginia

Room 426, Federal Bldg.
200 Granby Mall
Norfolk 23510

Room 10-020
400 North Eighth St.
Richmond 23240

Room 420, Poff Federal Bldg. and
U.S. Courthouse
210 Franklin Rd., SW.
Roanoke 24011

Washington

500 Century Tower Bldg.
1520 Third Ave.
Seattle 98101

Room 125
U.S. Courthouse
West 920 Riverside
Spokane 99201

Suite 415
Tacoma Mall Office Bldg.
2000 Tacoma Mall
Tacoma 98409

Room 305
U.S. Post Office Bldg.
25 South Third
Yakima 98901

West Virginia

Room B-006, Federal Court Bldg.
400 Neville St.
Beckley 25801

Room 3012, Federal Bldg.
500 Quarrier St.
Charleston 25301

Room 201, Post Office Bldg.
500 West Pike St.
Clarksburg 26302

Room 2701, Federal Bldg.
425 Juliani St.
Parkersburg 26101

Wisconsin

Room 303
212 East Washington Ave.
Madison 53703

Room 600
342 North Water St.
Milwaukee 53203

Room 321, Main Lake Bldg.
425 Main St.
Racine 53403

Room 5, Wood County Courthouse
400 Market St.
Wisconsin Rapids 54494

Wyoming

Rooms 4213–4215
Federal Bldg.
100 East B St.
Casper 82601

Room 8017
J.C. O'Mahoney Federal Center
2120 Capital Ave.
Cheyenne 82001

14

Job Outlook For
The 1980s

One statement about the future can be made with absolute certainty. It will be different from today. Constant change is the most significant aspect of the U.S. job market. Changes in the population, new technology and types of business, and changes in the needs and tastes of the public continually alter the economy and affect employment in all occupations. The population growth and the need for more medical care, education and other services and goods will increase the need for additional workers in those areas.

The computer, for example, has given birth to an entirely new group of occupations—programmers, systems analysts, equipment operators—while at the same time it has decreased the need for bookkeepers and certain kinds of clerical workers. Changes in the way businesses are organized and managed have had similar effects.

As an individual planning a career, your interests and abilities will determine the occupations that attract you, but future economic and social conditions will determine the job opportunities you will have. Fortunately, many factors that alter the demand for workers in occupations generally take place over a period of years. These include shifts in population or the labor force, the introduction of technology and the development of new organization and management techniques.

By examining what has happened in the past, it is possible to project some future requirements. Although no one can forecast the future with certainty, these employment projections will help you learn about future opportunities in occupations that interest you.

The information on industries and occupations covered here was, in part, obtained from the most recent edition of the *Occupational Outlook Handbook* published by the Bureau of Labor Statistics, U.S. Department of Labor, which in its entirety describes over fifty job categories and over 300 individual occupations. Information provided includes nature of the work, working conditions, places of employment, training, qualifications, earnings and sources of additional information. The handbook is for sale from the Superintendent of Documents, U.S. Government Printing Office, Washington, DC 20202. The price at this writing is about $12.50. It can also be found at most branches of your local public library.

Services—Fastest Growth Industry

Employment in service industries has been increasing at a faster rate than employment in manufacturing industries. Among the factors that have contributed to this rapid growth are rising incomes and living standards, resulting in greater demand for education, health care, entertainment and financial services. Because many services involve personal contact, people are less likely to be replaced by machines in service industries.

Employment in the service industries is expected to reach about 79 million workers in 1990—about 30 percent more than were employed in 1980. Growth will vary among industries within the group. The following is a summary of trends and projections of employment in some of the sectors that make up the service industries.

Accounting

Due to increasing pressure on businesses to improve budgeting and accounting procedures, demand for accountants will rise, as managers rely increasingly on accounting information to make business decisions. Plant expansion, mergers or foreign investments may depend upon specific financial considerations. Small businesses are expected to rely more on the expertise of public accountants in planning their operations.

Demand for college graduates with accounting degrees will be greater than for applicants who lack this training. Opportunities for accountants without college degrees will occur mainly in small businesses.

Many employers prefer graduates who have worked part-time in a business or accounting firm while in school. Experience has become so important that some employers seek persons with one or two years of experience for beginning positions. The increasing use of computers and electronic data processing systems in accounting should stimulate the demand for those trained in such procedures.

Banking

Through the 1980s bank employment is expected to increase much faster than the average for all occupations. Rising costs due to expanded banking services and the increasing dependence on computers will require more officers to provide sound management.

Greater international trade and investment will stimulate international and domestic banking activities, thus increasing the need for bank officers and managers. Opportunities will also increase as experienced officers leave their jobs. College graduates who meet the standard for management trainees should find good opportunities for entry-level positions.

Collection

One area of credit is expected to continue to increase. Because of the inflationary trends of prices on all goods and services, more and more people get into long-term debt, and in an unstable economy, often find themselves unable to meet their contractual obligations. Collection activities are an integral part of the credit system and positions in this segment of the credit field are expected to increase.

Credit

In the years ahead, businesses can be expected to require increasing amounts of credit to secure raw materials for production and obtain finished goods for resale. It is in the area of business credit where demand for credit managers will be strongest.

Consumers are expected to finance greater numbers of high-priced items. In addition, the use of credit for everyday purchases is expected to grow as demand increases for recreation and household goods as well as for consumer services. The use of computers for storing and retrieving information enables this greater volume of credit information to be processed more efficiently, and the use of telecommunications networks enables retail outlets to have immediate access to a central credit office.

However, the growth in the number of jobs for credit managers will be slowed due to the increased use of bank credit cards for consumer purchases. As stores substitute bank credit cards for their own charge accounts, retail store credit departments may be reduced.

Data Processing

Changes in data processing technology will have differing effects on computer operating occupations over the next decade. Employment of equipment operators is expected to rise, while employment of keypunch operators should continue to decline.

Recent advances in miniaturization of circuits have enabled manufacturers to reduce both the size and the cost of computer components. This will result in expansion in the use of computers, especially by small businesses. Employment of console equipment operators in data processing service firms may grow less rapidly than in the past as many small firms install their own equipment.

Employment of programmers is expected to grow faster than the average for all occupations during the 1980s as computer use expands, particularly in firms providing accounting and business management services. Many vacancies will be created as experienced workers transfer into jobs as systems analysts and managers.

The demand for applications programmers will increase as processes once done by hand are automated, but employment will not grow as rapidly as in the past for several reasons. Improved software that can be used by other than specially trained data processing personnel will simplify or eliminate some programming tasks.

Employment of programmers in data processing firms is not expected to rise as fast as in recent years. Technology has reduced both the size and cost of computer hardware, bringing computer systems within the reach of small businesses. As more small firms install their own computers rather than rely on data processing firms, employment growth in these data processing firms may slow.

Demand, however, should remain strong over the next decade. Prospects should be brightest for college graduates who have had computer-related courses, particularly for those with a major in computer science or a related field. Graduates of a two-year program in data processing also should find ample opportunities, although generally limited to business applications.

Economics

Business and industry, research organizations and consulting firms will continue to provide the largest number of employment opportunities for economists. This is due to the complexity of domestic and international economics and increased reliance on quantitative methods of analyzing business trends and forecasting sales. Employers will seek economists well trained in econometrics and statistics.

The need for economic analysis on the part of accountants, engineers, health administrators, urban planners and others will also contribute to an increase in the number of jobs for economists. Financial institutions and banking organizations will continue to have openings for well-educated, trained economists on all levels. Employment of economists in the federal government is expected to rise slowly—in line with the limited rate of growth projected for the federal work force as a whole.

Little or no employment growth is expected in colleges and universities, the traditional employers of many highly qualified economists. As a result, many such economists are expected to enter nonacademic positions.

Engineering

Much of the expected growth in requirements for engineers will stem from the development of defense-related products, scientific instruments, industrial machinery and chemical products. Opportunities in energy-related resources continue to decline. Engineers will also be needed to solve environmental problems although interest in environmental control has waned in the past few years.

Since the number of degrees expected to be granted in engineering in the 1980s is substantially higher than the number granted recently, some graduates may experience competition for engineering employment if the economy enters a recession. Engineering disciplines related to computer science will be in demand as the trend toward computerization in business and science increases.

Over the long run, the number of people seeking jobs as engineers is expected to be in balance with the number of job openings.

Health Care

Employment of health services administrators is expected to grow much faster than the average for all occupations in the 1980s as the quantity of patient services increases and health service management becomes more complex. This demand will be stimulated by the formation of more group medical practices and health maintenance organizations. Administrators will also be needed in nursing and convalescent homes to handle the increasing amount of administrative work expected as these facilities expand.

Hospitals and other patient care facilities will require nurses, aides, technicians, paraprofessionals, administrators and financial analysts for some time to come.

Research and development in biological science will continue to require more trained people in laboratory work, marketing and sales.

Journalism

The last two decades have shown a decrease in the number of metropolitan newspapers due to mergers and bankruptcies. Small-town and suburban daily or weekly newspapers have taken up some of the slack, but the prospects for newspaper reporters is bleak.

Small-town and suburban papers are expected to continue to offer the best opportunities for beginning reporters. Journalism graduates who are willing to relocate and start at relatively low salaries are likely to find reporting jobs on these newspapers. Openings arise on small papers as reporters gain experience and move up or transfer to reporting jobs on larger newspapers.

Because enrollments in journalism education programs are expected to rise through the 1980s, college teaching opportunities are expected to be good for qualified applicants with practical reporting experience. The favorable outlook for journalism educators contrasts with the generally bleak prospect for college faculty positions in many other academic disciplines.

Journalism graduates will find sufficient opportunities in other areas of communication, such as magazines, corporate communications, public relations and financial and business communications.

Library Work

The employment outlook for librarians is expected to remain competitive through the 1980s. The number of new graduates and labor force reentrants seeking jobs will probably exceed openings, with most job openings during the 1980s resulting from replacement needs.

Employment growth in public libraries is likely to be slower than it has been during the last two decades. Faced with escalating costs and tighter operating budgets, many libraries are expected to increase the use of volunteers, which will slow employment growth for librarians.

No growth is seen for academic librarians, a reflection of the decline in college enrollments expected during the 1980s. In school libraries, very modest growth is foreseen. Opportunities will be best for librarians with scientific and technical backgrounds, particularly in private libraries in the health sciences area. The expanding use of computers to store information and to handle routine operations will sustain the demand for information specialists.

Marketing

The marketing department of a company is one of the key profit centers. It encompasses all of the activities, including sales, that ultimately move goods or services to the final customer.

Therefore, the need for college graduates with degrees in marketing and business will continue to grow during the 1980s as it has done in past decades. Larger corporations demand M.B.A.'s for their entry-level positions, and those graduates from top-rated colleges and universities are offered the highest starting salaries.

Smaller firms will accept undergraduate degrees but they offer less money to start. Those without degrees will find marketing positions generally closed to them.

Because marketing executives are considered the prime profit-makers in a corporation, their salaries are among the highest in the corporate structure, and a large percentage of chief operating officers come from the marketing department.

Marketing Research

Opportunities should be best for applicants with training in marketing research. The growing complexity of marketing research techniques also may expand opportunities in this field for economists.

Marketing research employment rises as new products and services are developed, particularly when business activity and personal incomes are expanding rapidly. In periods of slow economic growth, however, the reduced demand for marketing services may limit the hiring of research workers.

Population growth and the increased variety of goods and services that businesses and people will require are expected to stimulate a high level of marketing activity. As a result, employment of marketing research workers is expected to grow much faster than the average for all occupations through the 1980s.

Office and Clerical

Employment of clerical workers is expected to maintain its present levels, resulting primarily in an increase in paperwork. Although a great deal of paperwork is handled by computers, and automation has had a strong impact on office equipment, computerization will not affect all clerical jobs. Demand will continue to be strong in banking, insurance and manufacturing and in firms that provide business, professional, health or educational services.

The demand for secretaries will continue to increase and the 1980s will see no change in that trend. The acute shortage of secretaries is being further enhanced by the reluctance of women and men to do secretarial work. Although automation can accomplish some of the work done by secretaries, traditional skills are still required for efficient office administration.

Personnel

Legislation setting standards in areas of occupational safety and health, equal employment opportunity and pensions has stimulated demand for personnel workers. The increasing size of companies due to mergers and acquisitions and the complexity of labor-management relations will ensure the need for trained people in the areas of recruitment, labor relations, wage and salary administration, executive compensation and benefits administration.

For positions in the personnel departments of large corporations, a bachelor's degree is the minimum qualification necessary. Personnel is one field where a liberal arts education is not a deterrent to hiring, although degrees in business administration, psychology or industrial relations are preferable. It is possible for noncollege graduates to enter the personnel field in smaller companies by obtaining a position as personnel clerk or assistant, and advancing to more responsible positions.

Public Relations

Employment of public relations people is expected to increase during the 1980s. However, demand for public relations personnel may slacken as employers delay expansion or cut their staffs during business slowdowns. Over the long run, corporations, associations, public relations agencies and other large organizations are expected to expand their public relations staffs.

Competition for beginning jobs is keen, for the glamour and excitement of public relations attracts large numbers of job seekers, including transfers from newspapers, advertising and closely related jobs.

Prospects for a career in public relations are best for highly qualified applicants—talented people with sound academic preparation and some media experience. Most openings are expected to occur in large organizations, corporations, public relations consulting firms, manufacturing firms and educational institutions.

Purchasing

Purchasing agents will continue to be in demand, as their importance in reducing costs is recognized. In large industrial organizations, the purchasing department will be expanded to handle the growing complexity of manufacturing processes. There will be a growing need for persons with a technical background to select highly technical goods.

Opportunities should also arise in firms providing personal, business and professional services. Strong growth is expected for this sector of the economy as a growing number of hospitals, school districts and other small employers are recognizing the importance of professional purchasing agents in reducing their operating costs.

Opportunities will be good for persons who have a master's degree in business administration, or a bachelor's degree in engineering, science or business administration whose college program included courses in purchasing.

Graduates of a two-year community college in purchasing should continue to find ample opportunities, although they will probably be limited to small firms.

Real Estate

In order to satisfy a growing demand for housing and other properties in the 1980s, employment of real estate agents and brokers is expected to rise. Also, replacement needs are high because a relatively large number of people transfer to other work after a short time of selling real estate.

The favorable outlook for employment in this field will stem primarily from increased demand for home purchases and rental units. Shifts in the age distribution of the population over the next decade will result in a larger number of young adults with careers and family responsibilities. This is the most geographically mobile group in our society and the one that traditionally makes the bulk of home purchases.

During periods of declining economic activity and tight credit, the volume of sales and the resulting demand for salespeople may decline and the number of persons seeking sales positions may outnumber openings. Over the long run, however, the outlook for salespeople is excellent.

Many opportunities should occur for both college graduates and mature workers transferring from other kinds of work. The field will remain highly competitive and prospects will be best for well-trained, ambitious people who enjoy selling. The proportion of part-time real estate agents has declined in recent years as brokers have demanded greater skill and professionalism from those selling real estate. This decline is expected to continue as agents need more specialized knowledge to handle real estate transactions.

Sociology

Employment for sociologists is expected to increase more slowly than the average for all occupations through the 1980s. Most openings will result from deaths, retirements and other separations from the labor force. Some academic openings may result from the growing trend to add sociology courses to the curriculum.

Demand in nonteaching areas will center around the increasing involvement of sociologists in the evaluation and administration of programs designed to cope with social and welfare problems.

Due to cut-backs in government social programs at all levels, the decrease in private donations to social service organizations and the decrease of available jobs for teachers in the public school systems, the number of jobs for college graduates with degrees in sociology will be smaller than in past decades. More opportunities, however, are opening up in the private sector, particularly in marketing areas.

Statistics

Employment opportunities for people who combine training in statistics with knowledge of applications are expected to be favorable through the 1980s with a faster than average growth pattern.

Private industry will require increasing numbers of statisticians for quality control in manufacturing. Statisticians with knowledge of engineering and physical science will find work with scientists and engineers in research and development. Business firms will rely more heavily than in the past on statisticians to forecast sales, analyze business conditions, modernize accounting procedures and help solve management problems.

Many fields such as law, finance and urban planning recognize the usefulness of statistics, and statistical techniques are being used increasingly in all areas of business and government. As the use of statistics expands into new areas, more statisticians will be needed.

Summing Up

- The fastest growth industries for the 1980s will be those providing services.
- Health care will continue to be among the fastest growing services.
- Proposed increased defense spending will require more engineers, scientists and industrial workers to be added

to the work force of prime government contractors and subcontractors.

- Despite the growth of automated offices, the shortage of secretaries will remain critical while salaries of experienced secretaries will reach new heights.
- Financial services (accounting, banking) will expand and require more highly trained workers to handle the increased complexities of business.
- The demand for data processing specialists will reach new highs in the 1980s due to the rapid growth of new technology.
- Those with degrees and training in sociology will face a decline in the need for their services in the 1980s.
- Journalism students will find fewer jobs and more competition than ever before with the increases of journalism school enrollments and the decrease in newspapers.
- Opportunities in marketing will continue to increase during the 1980s.

15

You're Hired

"Report for work on Monday."

These are the words you have been hoping to hear since you began your job search. Whether it took you two months, six months or what seems like forever, you have been offered and you have accepted a position.

All the frustration, aggravation and constant hustling is behind you. Ahead of you now is a new set of problems to be solved, but at least you'll be getting paid for it.

Thank Your Helpers

While you're patting yourself on the back congratulating yourself on how clever you were to get the job you wanted, don't forget some of the people who helped you along the way—those who gave you encouragement when your bottom was dragging, sympathy when your feet and your ego hurt, advice when you didn't know how to start your résumé, names of people to contact when you thought you were all alone in the world and comfort when you were ready to join the Foreign Legion. And just don't remember them in your mind. Show them in a tangible but simple way that you are grateful for their help.

Use your newly learned letter-writing skills to thank each one for his or her help. Write a note to those who showed you some concern, courtesy and kindness when none of these were in abundance—employment agency counselors who made an effort for you (without charge), company recruiters or personnel people who gave you the opportunity to present your qualifications, professors and teachers who advised you, and friends and relatives who held your hand when the prospects seemed bleakest.

Your thoughtfulness will make you and them feel good and, from a practical point of view, may bear fruit sometime in the future should you be in a similar position.

At the end of this chapter are some letters you can use as examples.

Your First Days

The purpose of this book was to try to help you get your first job and not to tell you how to handle yourself once you became a member of the working class. However, a few words are in order about some of the situations you may run into.

As the new kid on the block, don't expect to be greeted by the welcome wagon. You'll be lucky if anyone notices you for a day or two. Your first permanent job in a strange environment can be lonely. You are no longer among your peers. The people you are thrown in with will have little in common with you. They will generally be older, have more experience and, with a few exceptions, probably treat you as an outsider for a little while.

Don't take it personally. It is a natural reaction and happens all the time. Your first days will probably be bewildering. Finding your way to the washroom for the first time will be a major accomplishment. But by the end of the first week, you will have gotten your bearings, made a few friends and will feel as if you really belong. That's when it all becomes worthwhile—especially on payday.

You may be in for another shock when you go into a new job. One of the people who interviewed you for the job will probably be your immediate boss. You may have been impressed with his or her gentleness, kindness and understanding at the interview. But be prepared for another side when you report for work. You have changed from a job candidate to an employee and as such you are a subordinate, an underling, a part of the furniture, if you will. After having spent most of your life in school preparing for the big time, finding yourself at the bottom of the totem pole can be a shock.

You're not the first. Everyone has been there before. You'll get your chance at success, but you have to pay your dues first.

Accept your trivial assignments with grace, good humor and patience. It's part of your training. Someday you will be sitting in the walnut paneled office watching the new trainees perform the same routine, dull, unpleasant tasks.

Summing Up

- Be sure and thank all the people who helped you along the way.
- Send each one a personal note of appreciation.
- It's not only the correct thing to do, but you may need their help again some day.
- Your first days on the new job can be difficult.
- Your duties will probably be menial at the beginning.
- Be patient, everyone starts at the bottom.

Thank You Letters

Janet Oster
1411 Tremont Avenue
Bronx, NY 10942

March 17, 1983

Mr. James Alverez
45 W. 75th Street
New York, NY 10023

Dear Jim:

I am pleased to report that I start my new job with the Heller Advertising Agency next week, and I want to thank you for your valuable help.

I contacted some of the companies you recommended and although my job is not with one of them, your introductions did help me get interviews.

Your kindness and cooperation in spending your time and effort on my behalf is very much appreciated.

Cordially,

Janet Oster

Frank Baron
1326 Central Avenue
Pittsburgh, PA 17261

January 16, 1983

Ms. Janice Davis
Director, Student Placement Office
Penn State University
State College, PA 17842

Dear Ms. Davis:

I want to express my appreciation to
you for the assistance given me in my job
campaign. Your help was instrumental in
my getting two job offers, one of which I
just accepted.

Your seminar "How To Prepare for the
Interview," was particularly helpful, and
contributed greatly to my success in finding
a job. All of the people who participated
in the job aid program were helpful and
showed a great deal of understanding.

Again, thank you for your help.

Sincerely,

Frank Baron

SUSAN FORREST
19 Frommer Avenue
San Francisco, CA 94208
(914) 555-8974

June 29, 1983

Janice Michaels
CMA Employment Agency
145 River Road
San Francisco, CA 94101

Dear Ms. Michaels:

   Because of your continuing interest in my
career prospects and your efforts to help me
locate a position, I am writing now to advise
you that I shall be joining the Financial Services
Division of the Bank of America on August 1st.

   Thank you for your expert assistance and
encouragement.

                              Sincerely,

                              Susan Forrest

Appendix 1

Occupational Data

The following information on approximately 300 occupations in all fields has been reprinted from *The Occupational Outlook Quarterly*, published by the Bureau of Labor Statistics, United States Department of Labor.

It provides a concise description of the educational requirements for each occupation plus information on aptitudes, qualifications and working conditions.

	High school	Tech. sch/Apprenticeship trng.	Junior college	College	Problem-solving ability	Uses tools, machinery	Instructs others	Repetitious work	Hazardous	Outdoors	Physical stamina	Generally confined	Precision	Works with detail	Frequent public contact	Part-time	Able to see results	Creativity	Influences others	Competition on the job	Works as part of a team	Jobs widely scattered	Initiative
	1	2	3	4	5	6	7	8	9	10	11	12	13	14	15	16	17	18	19	20	21	22	23

INDUSTRIAL PRODUCTION AND RELATED OCCUPATIONS

Foundry occupations

	1	2	3	4	5	6	7	8	9	10	11	12	13	14	15	16	17	18	19	20	21	22	23
Patternmakers	•	A			•						•	•	•	•			•					•	
Molders		A			•		•	•			•	•					•					•	
Coremakers		A			•			•			•	•	•				•					•	

Machining occupations

	1	2	3	4	5	6	7	8	9	10	11	12	13	14	15	16	17	18	19	20	21	22	23
All-round machinists	•	A			•	•		•			•	•	•	•			•					•	
Instrument makers (mechanical)	•	A			•	•					•	•	•				•	•			•	•	
Machine tool operators					•	•		•	•		•	•	•				•					•	
Setup workers (machine tools)	•	A			•	•		•			•	•	•				•					•	
Tool-and-die makers	•	A			•	•					•	•	•				•					•	

Printing occupations

	1	2	3	4	5	6	7	8	9	10	11	12	13	14	15	16	17	18	19	20	21	22	23
Compositors	•	A			•						•	•	•				•					•	
Lithographers	•	A			•						•	•	•				•	•				•	
Photoengravers	•	A			•						•	•	•				•					•	
Electrotypers and stereotypers	•	A			•		•				•	•					•					•	
Printing press operators and assistants	•	A			•		•	•			•	•										•	
Bookbinders and bindery workers	•	A			•		•	•			•	•					•					•	

Other industrial production and related occupations

	1	2	3	4	5	6	7	8	9	10	11	12	13	14	15	16	17	18	19	20	21	22	23
Assemblers					•		•					•	•								•		
Automobile painters		A			•				•		•	•	•				•					•	
Blacksmiths		A			•		•	•	•		•	•						•	•			•	
Blue-collar worker supervisors	•	(1)	(1)	(1)	•		•							•					•	•	•	•	•
Boilermaking occupations		A			•	•	•	•	•		•		•				•					•	
Boiler tenders					•			•	•		•											•	
Electroplaters	•	A			•		•	•	•			•	•	•			•					•	
Forge shop occupations	(2)	(2)			•		•	•	•		•		•				•					•	
Furniture upholsterers					•		•				•	•					•	•				•	
Inspectors (manufacturing)			•		•		•				•	•	•									•	
Millwrights		A			•	•		•			•		•				•					•	
Motion picture projectionists					•		•					•				•						•	
Ophthalmic laboratory technicians	•				•		•					•	•									•	
Photographic laboratory occupations					•		•					•										•	
Power truck operators					•	•		•	•	•	•	•										•	
Production painters					•			•	•		•	•	•				•					•	
Stationary engineers		A		•	•				•		•											•	
Waste water treatment plant operators	•	(2)	(2)	(2)	•	•				•			•	•								•	•
Welders	•	T			•		•	•	•		•		•				•					•	

Notes appear at the end of the table

OFFICE OCCUPATIONS

	1 High school	2 Tech. sch/Apprenticeship trng.	3 Junior college	4 College	5 Problem-solving ability	6 Uses tools, machinery	7 Instructs others	8 Repetitious work	9 Hazardous	10 Outdoors	11 Physical stamina	12 Generally confined	13 Precision	14 Works with detail	15 Frequent public contact	16 Part-time	17 Able to see results	18 Creativity	19 Influences others	20 Competition on the job	21 Works as part of a team	22 Jobs widely scattered	23 Initiative
Clerical occupations																							
Bookkeeping workers	•							•				•	•	•		•	•				•	•	
Cashiers								•				•	•	•	•	•						•	
Collection workers	•							•				•		•	•					•	•	•	•
File clerks								•					•	•		•					•	•	
Hotel front office clerks	•				•		•	•				•		•	•						•	•	
Office machine operators	•					•		•				•	•	•							•	•	
Postal clerks						•		•			•	•	•									•	
Receptionists	•						•	•				•		•	•	•					•	•	
Secretaries and stenographers	•							•				•	•	•		•	•				•	•	
Shipping and receiving clerks						•		•			•	•	•									•	
Statistical clerks	•							•				•	•	•								•	
Stock clerks						•		•			•	•	•									•	
Typists	•							•				•	•	•		•	•					•	
Computer and related occupations																							
Computer operating personnel	•	T		•	•			•				•	•	•							•	•	
Programmers		(¹)	(¹)	(¹)	•							•	•	•							•	•	
Systems analysts				•	•		•					•	•	•									•
Banking occupations																							
Bank clerks	•							•				•	•	•							•	•	
Bank officers and managers			•	•		•						•	•	•	•				•		•	•	•
Bank tellers								•				•	•	•	•	•					•	•	
Insurance occupations																							
Actuaries				•	•							•	•	•								•	
Claim representatives			(¹)	(¹)	•		•				•	•	•	•								•	
Underwriters				•	•							•	•	•							•	•	
Administrative and related occupations																							
Accountants				•	•		•					•	•	•							•	•	
Advertising workers				•	•									•	•			•	•	•	•		•
Buyers				•	•									•					•	•	•		
City managers				+	•		•							•	•			•	•		•	•	•
College student personnel workers				•	•									•	•				•		•	•	
Credit managers				•	•		•					•	•	•					•		•	•	
Hotel managers and assistants				•	•		•							•	•				•		•	•	•
Industrial traffic managers		(¹)	(¹)	(¹)	•									•								•	
Lawyers				+	•		•							•	•			•	•	•		•	•
Marketing research workers				•	•								•	•				•	•			•	•
Personnel and labor relations workers				•	•		•							•	•			•			•	•	

	High school	Tech. sch/Apprenticeship trng.	Junior college	College	Problem-solving ability	Uses tools, machinery	Instructs others	Repetitious work	Hazardous	Outdoors	Physical stamina	Generally confined	Precision	Works with detail	Frequent public contact	Part-time	Able to see results	Creativity	Influences others	Competition on the job	Works as part of a team	Jobs widely scattered	Initiative
	1	2	3	4	5	6	7	8	9	10	11	12	13	14	15	16	17	18	19	20	21	22	23
Public relations workers				•	•									•	•			•	•	•	•	•	•
Purchasing agents				•	•									•							•	•	•
Urban planners				+	•									•	•			•	•		•	•	•
SERVICE OCCUPATIONS																							
Cleaning and related occupations																							
Building custodians					•		•				•			•								•	
Hotel housekeepers and assistants					•		•				•			•								•	
Pest controllers					•			•	•					•								•	
Food service occupations																							
Bartenders											•		•								•	•	
Cooks and chefs		(²)	(²)		•						•		•				•	•	•			•	
Dining room attendants and dishwashers								•						•	•						•	•	
Food counter workers								•			•		•	•	•						•	•	
Meatcutters		A			•			•	•		•		•	•			•					•	
Waiters and waitresses								•					•	•	•						•	•	
Personal service occupations																							
Barbers		T			•			•			•		•	•	•	•	•					•	
Bellhops and bell captains								•			•			•	•						•	•	
Cosmetologists		T			•			•			•		•	•	•	•	•					•	•
Funeral directors and embalmers	•	T			•				•					•	•							•	•
Private household service occupations																							
Private household workers					•		•				•						•					•	
Protective and related service occupations																							
Correction officers	•						•	•	•		•	•		•					•			•	•
FBI special agents			•	•	•		•		•		•			•					•				•
Firefighters	•				•	•		•	•	•	•			•							•		•
Guards							•	•	•	•	•	•											
Police officers	•				•		•	•	•	•	•			•	•				•		•		•
State police officers	•				•		•	•	•	•	•			•	•				•		•		•
Construction inspectors (Government)	•	T			•		•	•	•					•	•							•	•
Health and regulatory inspectors (Government)		(¹)	(¹)	(¹)	•		•	•						•	•						•	•	•
Occupational safety and health workers		(¹)	(¹)		•		•	•						•	•						•	•	•
Other service occupations																							
Mail carriers							•			•	•			•								•	•

	High school	Tech. sch/Apprenticeship trng.	Junior college	College	Problem-solving ability	Uses tools, machinery	Instructs others	Repetitious work	Hazardous	Outdoors	Physical stamina	Generally confined	Precision	Works with detail	Frequent public contact	Part-time	Able to see results	Creativity	Influences others	Competition on the job	Works as part of a team	Jobs widely scattered	Initiative
	1	2	3	4	5	6	7	8	9	10	11	12	13	14	15	16	17	18	19	20	21	22	23
Telephone operators	•					•	•	•				•			•							•	
EDUCATION AND RELATED OCCUPATIONS																							
Teaching occupations																							
Kindergarten and elementary school teachers			•	•	•		•							•	•			•	•		•	•	•
Secondary school teachers			•	•	•		•							•	•			•	•		•	•	•
College and university teachers			+	•	•		•							•	•			•	•		•	•	•
Teacher aides	•													•	•	•							
Library occupations																							
Librarians			+	•										•	•	•	•	•			•	•	•
Library technicians and assistants	•	T					•							•	•	•	•				•		
SALES OCCUPATIONS																							
Automobile parts counter workers	•					•	•				•				•							•	
Automobile sales workers	•														•	•			•	•		•	
Automobile service advisors	•			•	•										•						•	•	
Gasoline service station attendants						•	•	•	•	•	•				•	•						•	
Insurance agents and brokers	(¹)		(¹)(¹)	•	•									•	•		•		•	•		•	•
Manufacturers' sales workers				•	•										•				•	•		•	•
Models								•			•				•						•	•	
Real estate agents and brokers	•	T		•	•					•				•	•	•	•		•	•		•	•
Retail trade sales workers	•						•				•			•	•	•	•				•	•	•
Route drivers							•			•					•						•	•	
Securities sales workers			•	•	•								•	•	•	•	•		•	•		•	•
Travel agents	•				•									•	•		•				•	•	•
Wholesale trade sales workers	•				•									•	•		•		•	•		•	•
CONSTRUCTION OCCUPATIONS																							
Bricklayers, stonemasons, and marble setters		A			•	•			•	•	•						•	•				•	
Carpenters					•	•			•	•	•						•	•				•	
Cement masons and terrazzo workers						•			•	•	•						•				•	•	
Construction laborers						•			•	•	•										•	•	
Drywall installers and finishers						•	•	•			•						•					•	
Electricians (construction)	•	A			•	•			•	•	•		•				•					•	
Elevator constructors	•				•	•			•		•		•				•					•	
Floor covering installers					•	•		•					•				•					•	
Glaziers	•	A			•	•			•		•						•				•	•	
Insulation workers						•		•	•		•						•					•	

	High school	Tech. sch/Apprenticeship trng.	Junior college	College	Problem-solving ability	Uses tools, machinery	Instructs others	Repetitious work	Hazardous	Outdoors	Physical stamina	Generally confined	Precision	Works with detail	Frequent public contact	Part-time	Able to see results	Creativity	Influences others	Competition on the job	Works as part of a team	Jobs widely scattered	Initiative
	1	2	3	4	5	6	7	8	9	10	11	12	13	14	15	16	17	18	19	20	21	22	23
Ironworkers						•			•	•	•						•				•	•	
Lathers						•		•									•					•	
Operating engineers (construction machinery operators)		T			•	•			•	•	•	•					•					•	
Painters and paperhangers						•		•	•	•	•	•			•		•					•	
Plasterers						•					•						•					•	
Plumbers and pipefitters	•	A			•	•			•	•	•		•		•		•					•	
Roofers						•			•	•	•						•				•	•	
Sheet-metal workers	•	A			•	•					•						•					•	
Tilesetters		A				•					•						•					•	

OCCUPATIONS IN TRANSPORTATION ACTIVITIES

Air transportation occupations

	1	2	3	4	5	6	7	8	9	10	11	12	13	14	15	16	17	18	19	20	21	22	23
Air traffic controllers	•	T			•				•				•	•	•						•	•	•
Airplane mechanics	•	T			•	•			•	•	•		•				•				•	•	
Airplane pilots	•	T			•	•							•	•							•	•	•
Flight attendants	•							•	•		•				•		•						
Reservation, ticket, and passenger agents	•				•			•	•				•	•	•						•	•	

Merchant marine occupations

	1	2	3	4	5	6	7	8	9	10	11	12	13	14	15	16	17	18	19	20	21	22	23
Merchant marine officers	•	T	•		•	•			•	•		•	•		•						•		•
Merchant marine sailors						•		•	•	•	•	•									•		

Railroad occupations

	1	2	3	4	5	6	7	8	9	10	11	12	13	14	15	16	17	18	19	20	21	22	23
Brake operators	•				•			•	•	•	•										•	•	
Conductors	•				•		•	•	•												•	•	•
Locomotive engineers	•				•	•		•			•										•	•	
Shop trades		A			•	•		•	•	•											•		
Signal department workers					•	•				•			•				•				•		
Station agents					•		•	•			•				•	•					•		•
Telegraphers, telephoners, and tower operators								•			•				•							•	•
Track workers						•			•	•	•						•					•	•

Driving occupations

	1	2	3	4	5	6	7	8	9	10	11	12	13	14	15	16	17	18	19	20	21	22	23
Intercity busdrivers					•			•			•				•							•	
Local transit busdrivers					•			•			•				•							•	
Local truckdrivers					•			•			•											•	
Long distance truckdrivers					•			•			•											•	
Parking attendants					•			•	•	•					•	•						•	
Taxicab driver					•			•		•	•				•	•						•	

SCIENTIFIC AND TECHNICAL OCCUPATIONS

	High school	Tech. sch/Apprenticeship trng.	Junior college	College	Problem-solving ability	Uses tools, machinery	Instructs others	Repetitious work	Hazardous	Outdoors	Physical stamina	Generally confined	Precision	Works with detail	Frequent public contact	Part-time	Able to see results	Creativity	Influences others	Competition on the job	Works as part of a team	Jobs widely scattered	Initiative
	1	2	3	4	5	6	7	8	9	10	11	12	13	14	15	16	17	18	19	20	21	22	23
Conservation occupations																							
Foresters				•	•				•	•	•										•	•	•
Forestry technicians		•				•			•	•	•											•	•
Range managers				•	•				•	•	•											•	•
Soil conservationists				•	•		•															•	•
Engineers																							
Aerospace				•	•								•	•			•	•			•		•
Agricultural				•	•								•	•			•	•			•	•	•
Biomedical				•	•								•	•			•	•			•	•	•
Ceramic				•	•								•	•			•	•			•	•	•
Chemical				•	•								•	•			•	•			•	•	•
Civil				•	•								•	•			•	•			•	•	•
Electrical				•	•								•	•			•	•			•	•	•
Industrial				•	•								•	•			•	•			•	•	•
Mechanical				•	•								•	•			•	•			•	•	•
Metallurgical				•	•								•	•			•	•			•	•	•
Mining				•	•								•	•			•	•			•	•	•
Petroleum				•	•								•	•			•	•			•	•	•
Environmental scientists																							
Geologists				•	•	•				•			•	•				•				•	•
Geophysicists				•	•	•				•			•	•				•				•	•
Meteorologists				•	•	•							•	•				•				•	•
Oceanographers				+	•	•				•			•	•				•			•		•
Life science occupations																							
Biochemists				+	•	•							•	•				•				•	•
Life scientists				+	•	•							•	•				•				•	•
Soil scientists				•	•	•							•	•								•	•
Mathematics occupations																							
Mathematicians				•	•								•	•				•				•	•
Statisticians				•	•								•	•				•				•	•
Physical scientists																							
Astronomers				+	•	•							•	•				•				•	•
Chemists				•	•	•							•	•				•				•	•
Food scientists				•	•	•							•	•				•				•	•
Physicists				+	•	•							•	•				•				•	•
Other scientific and technical occupations																							
Broadcast technicians	•	T		•	•								•	•	•							•	
Drafters	•	T		•	•	•		•					•	•		•						•	•
Engineering and science technicians	•	T		•	•								•	•								•	•
Surveyors	•	T			•					•	•		•	•								•	•

MECHANICS AND REPAIRERS

	1 High school	2 Tech. sch/Apprenticeship trng.	3 Junior college	4 College	5 Problem-solving ability	6 Uses tools, machinery	7 Instructs others	8 Repetitious work	9 Hazardous	10 Outdoors	11 Physical stamina	12 Generally confined	13 Precision	14 Works with detail	15 Frequent public contact	16 Part-time	17 Able to see results	18 Creativity	19 Influences others	20 Competition on the job	21 Works as part of a team	22 Jobs widely scattered	23 Initiative
Telephone craft occupations																							
Central office craft occupations					•	•			•				•				•					•	
Central office equipment installers					•	•			•		•		•				•					•	
Line installers and cable splicers					•	•			•	•	•											•	
Telephone and PBX installers and repairers					•	•																	•
Other mechanics and repairers																							
Air-conditioning, refrigeration, and heating mechanics	•				•	•			•								•					•	
Appliance repairers	•				•	•			•						•		•					•	
Automobile body repairers		A			•	•			•			•	•									•	
Automobile mechanics		A			•	•			•		•	•	•				•					•	
Boat-engine mechanics					•	•			•		•	•					•					•	
Bowling-pin-machine mechanics					•	•		•	•		•											•	
Business machine repairers	•	T			•	•			•				•				•					•	•
Computer service technicians	•	T			•	•			•				•				•					•	•
Diesel mechanics		A			•	•			•		•	•	•				•					•	•
Electric sign repairers	•				•	•			•	•					•		•					•	
Farm equipment mechanics		A			•	•			•	•	•						•					•	
Industrial machinery repairers		A			•	•			•		•						•					•	
Instrument repairers	•	A			•	•					•						•					•	
Jewelers	•	A			•	•							•	•			•	•				•	•
Locksmiths					•	•							•		•		•					•	
Maintenance electricians	•	A			•	•			•				•				•					•	
Motorcycle mechanics					•	•			•			•					•					•	
Piano and organ tuners and repairers	•	T			•	•								•		•	•					•	
Shoe repairers					•			•	•		•	•					•					•	•
Television and radio service technicians		T			•	•			•				•				•					•	•
Truck mechanics and bus mechanics		A			•	•			•		•	•	•				•					•	
Vending machine mechanics					•	•		•	•								•					•	•
Watch repairers		T			•	•							•	•								•	•

HEALTH OCCUPATIONS

	1	2	3	4	5	6	7	8	9	10	11	12	13	14	15	16	17	18	19	20	21	22	23
Dental occupations																							
Dentists			+		•	•	•						•				•	•	•	•	•	•	•
Dental assistants	•	T				•	•	•							•	•	•				•	•	•
Dental hygienists			•		•	•	•						•		•	•	•				•	•	•
Dental laboratory technicians			(³)	(³)	•	•		•					•	•							•	•	
Medical practitioners																							
Chiropractors			+		•	•	•				•		•		•		•	•	•		•	•	•

	High school	Tech. sch/Apprenticeship trng.	Junior college	College	Problem-solving ability	Uses tools, machinery	Instructs others	Repetitious work	Hazardous	Outdoors	Physical stamina	Generally confined	Precision	Works with detail	Frequent public contact	Part-time	Able to see results	Creativity	Influences others	Competition on the job	Works as part of a team	Jobs widely scattered	Initiative
	1	2	3	4	5	6	7	8	9	10	11	12	13	14	15	16	17	18	19	20	21	22	23
Optometrists				+	•	•	•				•		•	•	•	•	•		•		•	•	•
Osteopathic physicians				+	•	•	•		•		•		•	•			•		•		•	•	•
Physicians				+	•	•	•		•		•		•	•			•		•		•	•	•
Podiatrists				+	•	•	•				•		•	•			•		•		•	•	•
Veterinarians				+	•	•	•		•		•		•	•			•		•		•	•	•
Medical technologist, technician, and assistant occupations																							
Electrocardiograph technicians	•	T				•	•	•					•	•	•	•					•	•	
Electroencephalographic technologists and technicians	•	T				•	•	•					•	•	•						•	•	
Emergency medical technicians	•	T		•	•	•	•		•	•	•		•	•	•						•	•	
Medical laboratory workers	•	(²)	(²)	(²)	•		•	•				•	•	•							•	•	
Medical record technicians and clerks	•	(²)	(²)				•					•	•	•							•	•	
Operating room technicians		(³)	(³)		•	•	•	•				•	•	•							•	•	
Optometric assistants	•				•	•						•	•	•							•	•	
Radiologic (X-ray) technologists		•			•	•	•		•			•	•	•								•	
Respiratory therapy workers	•	(²)	(²)	(²)	•	•						•	•	•							•	•	
Nursing occupations																							
Registered nurses	(⁴)	(⁴)	(⁴)	•	•	•		•			•		•	•	•	•	•		•		•	•	•
Licensed practical nurses		T			•	•		•			•		•	•	•	•	•		•		•	•	
Nursing aides, orderlies, and attendants					•	•	•	•	•		•			•	•						•	•	
Therapy and rehabilitation occupations																							
Occupational therapists			•	•	•	•	•							•	•		•	•	•		•	•	•
Occupational therapy assistants		(²)	(²)		•	•								•	•	•	•		•		•	•	
Physical therapists			•	•	•	•	•				•			•	•		•	•	•		•	•	•
Physical therapist assistants and aides		(²)	(²)		•	•					•			•	•		•		•		•	•	
Speech pathologists and audiologists				+	•	•	•						•	•	•		•	•	•		•	•	•
Other health occupations																							
Dietitians			•	•		•							•	•	•	•		•			•	•	•
Dispensing opticians	•	A			•	•							•	•	•						•	•	
Health services administrators				+	•									•					•	•	•	•	•
Medical record administrators				•	•								•	•						•	•	•	•
Pharmacists				+	•		•					•	•	•	•						•	•	•
SOCIAL SCIENTISTS																							
Anthropologists				+	•		(⁵)						•	(⁵)			•				•	•	
Economists			•	•		(⁵)							•	(⁵)			•				•	•	
Geographers			•	•	•	(⁵)							•	(⁵)			•				•	•	
Historians				+	•		(⁵)						•	(⁵)			•				•	•	
Political scientists				+	•		(⁵)						•	•			•				•	•	•
Psychologists				+	•		•						•	•			•				•	•	
Sociologists				+	•		(⁵)						•	•			•				•	•	

1. Educational requirements vary by industry or employer.   2. Educational requirements vary according to type of work.

	High school	Tech. sch/Apprenticeship trng.	Junior college	College	Problem-solving ability	Uses tools, machinery	Instructs others	Repetitious work	Hazardous	Outdoors	Physical stamina	Generally confined	Precision	Works with detail	Frequent public contact	Part-time	Able to see results	Creativity	Influences others	Competition on the job	Works as part of a team	Jobs widely scattered	Initiative
	1	2	3	4	5	6	7	8	9	10	11	12	13	14	15	16	17	18	19	20	21	22	23
SOCIAL SERVICE OCCUPATIONS																							
Counseling occupations																							
School counselors				+	•		•							•	•			•	•		•	•	•
Employment counselors				+	•		•					•		•	•		•	•			•	•	
Rehabilitation counselors				+	•		•							•	•			•	•		•	•	
College career planning and placement counselors				+	•		•							•	•			•	•		•	•	•
Clergy																							
Protestant ministers				+	•		•								•			•		•	•		•
Rabbis				+	•		•								•			•	•	•	•		•
Roman Catholic priests				+	•		•								•			•	•		•		•
Other social service occupations																							
Cooperative extension service workers			•	•											•		•		•		•	•	•
Home economists			•	•											•			•	•		•		•
Homemaker-home health aides							•														•	•	
Park, recreation, and leisure service workers	•	(²)	(²)	(²)	•		•			•	•				•	•		•	•		•	•	•
Social service aides				•	•		•	•									•	•			•		•
Social workers			•	•	•		•								•		•	•	•		•	•	•
ART, DESIGN, AND COMMUNICATIONS-RELATED OCCUPATIONS																							
Performing artists																							
Actors and actresses		T					(⁵)				•				•		•	•		•	•		•
Dancers		T					(⁵)				•				•			•		•	•		•
Musicians		T					(⁵)				•				•	•		•		•	•		•
Singers		T					(⁵)				•				•			•		•	•		•
Design occupations																							
Architects			•	•	•								•	•	•		•	•	•	•	•	•	•
Commercial artists	•	T			•		•								•			•			•	•	•
Display workers	•						•											•			•	•	•
Floral designers												•		•				•			•		•
Industrial designers			•	•										•	•			•			•		•
Interior designers			•											•	•			•	•		•	•	•
Landscape architects			•	•										•	•			•	•		•		•
Photographers		(³)	(³)												•			•			•	•	•
Communications-related occupations																							
Interpreters				•			•						•	•									•
Newspaper reporters				•			•						•	•	•		•	•			•	•	•
Radio and television announcers			•				•					•			•			•	•		•		•
Technical writers				•	•		•							•				•					•

3. Training programs are available from vocational schools or junior colleges.
4. Diploma, baccalaureate, and associate degree programs prepare R.N. candidates for licensure. The baccalaureate degree is preferred for entry positions such as public health nurse, however, and is needed for advancement to supervisory positions or for clinical specialization.
5. Teachers only.

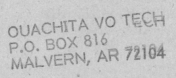

Appendix 2

Information Sources By Occupation

ACCOUNTING

Organizations
American Institute of CPAs
1211 Avenue of the Americas
New York, NY 10036

National Association of Accountants
919 Third Avenue
New York, NY 10022

National Society of Public Accountants
1717 Pennsylvania Avenue
Washington, DC 20006

Publications
CPA JOURNAL
600 Third Avenue
New York, NY 10016

JOURNAL OF ACCOUNTANCY
1211 Avenue of the Americas
New York, NY 10036

ADMINISTRATION

Organizations
Administrative Management Society
Willow Grove, PA 19090

American Management Association
135 West 50th Street
New York, NY 10020

Publications
CONFERENCE BOARD RECORD
845 Third Avenue
New York, NY 10022

MANAGEMENT REVIEW
135 West 50th Street
New York, NY 10020

MANAGEMENT WORLD
Maryland Road
Willow Grove, PA 19090

ADVERTISING

Organizations
Advertising Council
825 Third Avenue
New York, NY 10022

Advertising Research Foundation
3 East 54th Street
New York, NY 10022

Association of National Advertisers
155 East 44th Street
New York, NY 10017

Direct Mail/Marketing Association
6 East 43rd Street
New York, NY 10017

Publications
ADVERTISING AGE
740 Rush Street
Chicago, IL 60611

DIRECT MARKETING MAGA-
ZINE
224 Seventh Avenue
Garden City, NY 11530

MADISON AVENUE HANDBOOK
17 East 48th Street
New York, NY 10017

STANDARD RATE & DATA SER-
VICE
5201 Old Orchard Road
Skokie, IL 60076

(Publishers of general information for
advertising agencies and advertisers.
Separate directories for consumer
magazines, business magazines,
newspapers, radio and TV stations,
farm publications and other specialized media.)

ADVERTISING AGENCIES

Organizations
American Association of Advertising
Agencies
666 Third Avenue
New York, NY 10017

Publications
AAAA ROSTER
666 Third Avenue
New York, NY 10017

ADWEEK
820 Second Avenue
New York, NY 10017

MADISON AVENUE MAGAZINE
369 Lexington Avenue
New York, NY 10017

ARCHITECTURE

Organizations
American Institute of Architects
1735 New York Avenue, N.W.
Washington, DC 20006

Publications
ARCHITECTURAL RECORD
1221 Avenue of the Americas
New York, NY 10020

GETTING INTO ARCHITECTURE
American Institute of Architects
1735 New York Avenue, N.W.
Washington, DC 20006

BANKING

Organizations
American Bankers Association
1120 Connecticut Avenue, N.W.
Washington, DC 20036

National Association of Mutual Savings Banks
200 Park Avenue
New York, NY 10017

Publications
AMERICAN BANKER
525 West 42nd Street
New York, NY 10036

SAVINGS BANK JOURNAL
200 Park Avenue
New York, NY 10017

AMERICAN BANK DIRECTORY
6364 Warren Drive
Norcross, GA 30093

BOOK PUBLISHING

Organizations
Association of American Publishers
1 Park Avenue
New York, NY 10016

Publications
BOOK AND MAGAZINE PRODUC-
TION
425 Huehl Road
Northbrook, IL 60062

PUBLISHERS WEEKLY
1180 Avenue of the Americas
New York, NY 10036

LITERARY MARKET PLACE
1180 Avenue of the Americas
New York, NY 10036

CHEMICAL ENGINEERING

Organizations
American Chemical Society
1155 16th Street N.W.
Washington, DC 20036

American Institute of Chemical Engineers
345 East 47th Street
New York, NY 10017

Publications
CHEMICAL ENGINEERING
1221 Avenue of the Americas
New York, NY 10020

CHEMICAL ENGINEERING CATALOG
600 Summer Street
Stamford, CT 06904

COMMERCIAL ART

Organizations
Art Directors Club
488 Madison Avenue
New York, NY 10022

Publications
ART DIRECTOR
10 East 39th Street
New York, NY 10016

GRAPHICS, USA
120 East 56th Street
New York, NY 10022

ARTS & CRAFTS MARKET
9933 Alliance Road
Cincinnati, OH 45242

CREDIT

Organizations
National Association of Credit Management
475 Park Avenue South
New York, NY 10016

National Institute of Credit
3000 Marcus Avenue
Lake Success, NY 11040

Publications
CREDIT & FINANCIAL MANAGEMENT
475 Park Avenue South
New York, NY 10016

CREDIT WORLD
243 Lindbergh Boulevard
St. Louis, MO 63130

DATA PROCESSING

Organizations
American Federation of Information Processing Societies
1815 North Lynn Street
Arlington, VA 22209

Association for Computing Machinery
1133 Avenue of the Americas
New York, NY 10036

Data Processing Management Association
505 Busse Highway
Park Ridge, IL 60068

Publications
COMPUTERWORLD
375 Cochituate Road
Framingham, MA 01701

DATAMATION
666 Fifth Avenue
New York, NY 10019

ECONOMICS

Organizations
National Association of Business
Economists
28349 Chagrin Boulevard
Cleveland, OH 44122

Publications
AMERICAN ECONOMIC REVIEW
1313 21st Street South
Nashville, TN 37212

BUSINESS ECONOMICS CA-
REERS
28349 Chagrin Boulevard
Cleveland, OH 44122

ELECTRONICS

Organizations
Electronics Industries Association
2001 Eye Street
Washington, DC 20006

Publications
ELECTRONIC BUSINESS
221 Columbus Avenue
Boston, MA 02116

ELECTRONIC DESIGN
50 Essex Street
Rochelle Park, NJ 07662

ELECTRONICS
1221 Avenue of the Americas
New York, NY 10020

FINANCE

Organizations
Financial Executives Institute
633 Third Avenue
New York, NY 10017

Publications
BARRON'S NATIONAL BUSI-
NESS AND FINANCIAL WEEKLY
22 Cortland Street
New York, NY 10004

FINANCIAL EXECUTIVE
633 Third Avenue
New York, NY 10017

FINANCIAL WORLD
150 East 58th Street
New York, NY 10155

HOME ECONOMICS

Organizations
American Home Economics Association
2010 Massachusetts Avenue, NW
Washington, DC 20036

Publications
JOURNAL OF HOME ECONOM-
ICS
2010 Massachusetts Avenue NW
Washington, DC 20036

AHEA DIRECTORY
2010 Massachusetts Avenue, NW
Washington, DC 20036

HEALTH CARE

Organizations
American Hospital Association
840 North Lake Shore Drive
Chicago, IL 60611

Publications
HOSPITAL FINANCIAL MAN-
AGEMENT
1900 Spring Road
Oakbrook, IL 60521

HOSPITALS
211 East Chicago Avenue
Chicago, IL 60611

HOTEL AND MOTEL

Organizations
American Hotel & Motel Association
888 Seventh Avenue
New York, NY 10019

Publications
HOTEL AND MOTEL MANAGE-
MENT
757 Third Avenue
New York, NY 10017

HOTEL & MOTEL RED BOOK
888 Seventh Avenue
New York, NY 10019

INDUSTRIAL DESIGN

Organizations
Industrial Designers Society of America
1717 N Street, NW
Washington, DC 20036

Publications
DESIGN NEWS
221 Columbus Avenue
Boston, MA 01772

INDUSTRIAL DESIGN
717 Fifth Avenue
New York, NY 10022

MACHINE DESIGN
111 Chester Avenue
Cleveland, OH 44114

INSURANCE

Organizations
National Association of Independent
Insurers
2600 River Road
Des Plaines, IL 60018

American Alliance of Insurance
20 North Wacker Drive
Chicago, IL 60606

Insurance Information Institute
110 William Street
New York, NY 10038

Publications
BEST'S WEEKLY REVIEW
Ambest Road
Oldwick, NJ 08858

INSURANCE ADVOCATE
45 John Street
New York, NY 10038

INSURANCE WEEK
First National Bank Building
Seattle, WA 98154

JOURNALISM

Organizations
American Society of Newspaper Editors
1315 Sullivan Trail
Easton, PA 10020

INTERNATIONAL ASSOCIATION
OF BUSINESS COMMUNICA-
TORS
870 Market Street
San Francisco, CA 94102

American Newspaper Publishers As-
sociation
P.O. Box 17407
Dulles International Airport
Washington, DC 20041

American Society of Business Press
Editors
435 North Michigan Avenue
Chicago, IL 60611

Publications
THE QUILL
35 East Wacker Drive
Chicago, IL 60601

FOLIO
125 Elm Street
New Canaan, CT 06840

EDITOR & PUBLISHER
575 Lexington Avenue
New York, NY 10022

LIBRARY

Organizations
American Library Association
50 East Huron Street
Chicago, IL 60611

Special Libraries Association
235 Park Avenue South
New York, NY 10018

Publications
AMERICAN LIBRARIES
50 East Huron Street
Chicago, IL 60611

LIBRARY JOURNAL
1180 Avenue of the Americas
New York, NY 10036

WILSON LIBRARY BULLETIN
940 University Avenue
Bronx, NY 10452

MARKETING/MARKET RESEARCH

Organizations
American Marketing Association
222 South Riverside Plaza
Chicago, IL 60606

Publications
JOURNAL OF MARKETING RE-
SEARCH
222 West Riverside Plaza
Chicago, IL 60606

MARKETING & COMMUNICA-
TIONS
475 Park Avenue South
New York, NY 10016

ADVERTISING AGE
740 Rush Street
Chicago, IL 60611

INDUSTRIAL MARKETING
740 Rush Street
Chicago, IL 60611

PERSONNEL

Organizations
American Management Association
135 West 50th Street
New York, NY 10020

American Society for Training and
Development
600 Maryland Avenue, SW
Washington, DC 20024

American Society for Personal Administration
30 Park Drive
Berea, OH 44107

Publications
PERSONNEL ADMINISTRATOR
30 Park Drive
Berea, OH 44107

PERSONNEL JOURNAL
866 West 18th Street
Costa Mesa, CA 92627

TRAINING & DEVELOPMENT
JOURNAL
600 Maryland Avenue, SW
Washington, DC 20024

PHOTOGRAPHY

Organizations
Photographic Society of America
2005 Walnut Street
Philadelphia, PA 19103

Professional Photographers of America
1090 Executive Way
Des Plaines, IL 60018

Publications
INDUSTRIAL PHOTOGRAPHY
475 Park Avenue South
New York, NY 10016

PHOTOGRAPHIC TRADE NEWS
250 Fulton Avenue
Hempstead, NY 11550

PRINTING & GRAPHIC ARTS

Organizations
American Institute of Graphic Arts
1059 Third Avenue
New York, NY 10022

Printing Industries of America
1730 Lynn Street
Arlington, VA 22209

Publications
GRAPHIC ARTS MONTHLY
666 Fifth Avenue
New York, NY 10019

PRINTING TRADES BLUE BOOK
79 Madison Avenue
New York, NY 10003

PRINTING IMPRESSIONS
401 North Broad Street
Philadelphia, PA 19108

PUBLIC RELATIONS

Organizations
Public Relations Society of America
845 Third Avenue
New York, NY 10022

Publications
O'DWYER'S DIRECTORY OF
PUBLIC RELATIONS FIRMS
271 Madison Avenue
New York, NY 10016

PUBLIC RELATIONS JOURNAL
845 Third Avenue
New York, NY 10022

PUBLISHING— MAGAZINES

Organizations
American Business Press
205 East 42nd Street
New York, NY 10017

American Society of Magazine Editors
575 Lexington Avenue
New York, NY 10022

American Society of Business Press
Editors
435 North Michigan Avenue
Chicago, IL 60611

Publications
FOLIO: THE MAGAZINE FOR
MAGAZINE MANAGEMENT
125 Elm Street
New Canaan, CT 06840

STANDARD RATE & DATA SER-
VICE
5201 Old Orchard Road
Skokie, IL 60076
(Complete list of consumer and trade
magazines with data on circulation,
personnel, advertising rates, format
and mechanical requirements.)

RETAIL

Organizations
National Retail Merchants Association
100 West 31st Street
New York, NY 10001

Publications
CHAIN STORE EXECUTIVE
425 Park Avenue
New York, NY 10022

CHAIN STORE AGE
425 Park Avenue
New York, NY 10022

TELEVISION & RADIO

Organizations
National Association of Broadcasters
1771 N Street, NW
Washington, DC 20036

Television Bureau of Advertising
485 Lexington Avenue
New York, NY 10017

Publications
BROADCASTING
1735 DeSales Street, NW
Washington, DC 20036

CAREERS IN RADIO
National Association of Broadcasters
1771 N Street, NW
Washington, DC 20036

RADIO AND TELEVISION
WEEKLY
254 West 31st Street
New York, NY 10001

TRAVEL & TOURISM

Organizations
American Society of Travel Agents
(ASTA)
711 Fifth Avenue
New York, NY 10022

Publications
ASTA TRAVEL NEWS
488 Madison Avenue
New York, NY 10022

TRAVEL AGENT MAGAZINE
2 West 46th Street
New York, NY 10036

TRAVEL TRADE MAGAZINE
6 East 46th Street
New York, NY 10017

TRAVEL WEEKLY
1 Park Avenue
New York, NY 10016

Appendix 3

Helpful Guides and Directories

AFFIRMATIVE ACTION:
A GUIDE FOR THE PERPLEXED
Continuing Education Service
Michigan State University
East Lansing, MI 48824

COLLEGE PLACEMENT ANNUAL
65 East Elizabeth Avenue
Bethlehem, PA 18018

DIRECTORY OF COLLEGE RECRUITING
PERSONNEL
65 East Elizabeth Avenue
Bethlehem, PA 18018

DIRECTORY OF COUNSELING SERVICES
Two Skyline Place
5203 Leesburg Pike
Falls Church, VA 22041

DIRECTORY OF CORPORATE AFFILIA-
TIONS
National Register Publishing Co.
5201 Skokie Road
Skokie, IL 60077

DIRECTORY OF DIRECTORIES
Book Tower Building
Detroit, MI 48226

DIRECTORY OF RESOURCES FOR AFFIR-
MATIVE RECRUITMENT
Equal Employment Opportunity Commission
2401 E Street
Washington, DC 20506

ENCYLOPEDIA OF ASSOCIATIONS
Gale Research Company
Book Tower Building
Detroit, MI 48226

EQUAL RIGHTS HANDBOOK
Avon Books
959 Eighth Avenue
New York, NY 10019

FEDERAL JOB DIRECTORY
1619 Traske Road
Encinitas, CA 92024

FORTUNE DOUBLE 500 DIRECTORY
Fortune Magazine
1271 Avenue of the Americas
New York, NY 10020

JOB FACTSHEET LIST
Council for Career Planning
310 Madison Avenue
New York, NY 10022

JOB HUNTER'S GUIDE TO AMERICAN CIT-
IES
4 Brattle Street
Cambridge, MA 02138

MILLION DOLLAR DIRECTORY
Dun & Bradstreet Co.
99 Church Street
New York, NY 10007

MOODY'S INDUSTRIAL MANUAL
99 Church Street
New York, NY 10007

NATIONAL DIRECTORY OF WOMEN'S EM-
PLOYMENT PROGRAMS
1649 K Street
Washington, DC 20006

POOR'S REGISTER OF CORPORATIONS,
DIRECTORS AND EXECUTIVES
25 Broadway
New York, NY 10014

STANDARD DIRECTORY OF ADVERTIS-
ERS
National Register Publishing Co.
5201 Old Orchard Road
Skokie, IL 60076

SUMMER EMPLOYMENT DIRECTORY OF
THE U.S.
9933 Alliance Road
Cincinnati, OH 45242

THOMAS REGISTER OF AMERICAN MAN-
UFACTURERS
1 Penn Plaza
New York, NY 10001

U.S. INDUSTRIAL DIRECTORY
1200 Summer Street
Stamford, CT 06905

WHO'S WHO IN FINANCE AND INDUSTRY
200 East Ohio Street
Chicago, IL 60611

APPENDIX 4

Salary Chart

YEAR	MONTH	WEEK	YEAR	MONTH	WEEK
10000	833.33	192.33	19500	1625.00	375.00
10500	875.00	201.92	20000	1666.77	384.62
11000	916.67	211.54	20500	1708.33	394.23
11500	958.33	221.15	21000	1750.00	403.85
12000	1000.00	230.77	21500	1791.67	413.46
12500	1041.67	240.38	22000	1833.33	423.08
13000	1083.33	250.00	22500	1875.00	432.69
13500	1125.00	259.62	23000	1916.67	442.31
14000	1166.67	269.23	23500	1958.33	451.92
14500	1208.33	278.85	24000	2000.00	461.54
15000	1250.00	288.46	24500	2041.67	471.15
15500	1291.67	298.08	25000	2083.33	480.77
16000	1333.33	307.69	25500	2125.00	490.38
16500	1375.00	317.31	26000	2166.67	500.00
17000	1416.67	326.92	26500	2208.33	509.62
17500	1458.33	336.54	27000	2250.00	519.23
18000	1500.00	346.15	27500	2291.67	528.85
18500	1541.67	355.77	28000	2333.33	538.46
19000	1583.33	365.38	28500	2375.00	548.08

YEAR	MONTH	WEEK	YEAR	MONTH	WEEK
29000	2416.67	557.69	42000	3500.00	807.69
29500	2458.33	567.31	42500	3541.67	817.31
30000	2500.00	576.92	43000	3583.33	826.92
30500	2541.67	586.54	43500	3625.00	836.54
31000	2583.33	596.15	44000	3666.67	846.15
31500	2625.00	605.77	44500	3708.33	855.57
32000	2666.67	615.38	45000	3750.00	865.38
32500	2708.33	625.00	45500	3791.67	875.00
33000	2750.00	634.62	46000	3833.33	884.62
33500	2791.67	644.23	46500	3875.00	894.23
34000	2833.33	653.85	47000	3916.67	903.85
34500	2875.00	663.46	47500	3958.33	913.46
35000	2916.67	673.08	48000	4000.00	923.08
35500	2958.33	682.59	48500	4041.67	932.69
36000	3000.00	692.37	49000	4083.33	942.31
36500	3041.67	701.92	49500	4125.00	951.92
37000	3083.33	711.54	50000	4166.67	961.54
37500	3125.00	721.15	55000	4583.33	1057.69
38000	3166.67	730.77	60000	5000.00	1153.89
38500	3208.33	740.38	65000	5416.66	1250.00
39000	3250.00	750.00	70000	5833.33	1346.15
39500	3291.67	759.62	75000	6250.00	1442.30
40000	3333.33	769.23	80000	6666.66	1538.46
40500	3375.00	778.85	85000	7083.33	1634.61
41000	3416.67	788.46	90000	7500.00	1730.76
41500	3458.33	798.08	95000	7916.66	1826.92
			100000	8333.33	1923.07

BIBLIOGRAPHY

Asta, Patricia and Bernbach, Linda. *Test Your Vocational Aptitude*. New York: Arco Publishing, 1976.

Bostwick, Burdette. *Résumé Writing: A Comprehensive How-to-do-it Guide*. New York: Wiley, 1980.

Casewit, Curtis W. *Strategies for Getting the Job You Want Now*. New York: Pilot Books, 1976.

Corwen, Leonard. *Job Hunter's Handbook: How to Sell Yourself and Get the Job You Really Want*. New York: Arco Publishing, 1966.

_____. *Your Résumé: Key to a Better Job*. New York: Arco Publishing, 1975.

_____. *Your Job: Where To Find It—How To Get It*. New York: Arco Publishing, 1981.

Figler, Howard E. *Path: A Career Workbook for Liberal Arts Students*. Cranston, RI: The Carroll Press, 1979.

Fox, Marcia R. *Put Your Degree to Work: Job Hunting Success For The New Professional*. New York: W. W. Norton, 1979.

Ginn, Robert J. *The College Graduates Career Guide*. New York: Scribner's, 1981.

Gowdy, Eve. *Job Hunting With Employment Agencies*. New York: Barron, 1978.

Greco, Benedetto. *How To Get The Job That's Right For You*. Homewood, IL: Dow Jones-Irwin, 1981.

Haldane, Bernard and Jean, and Martin, Lowell. *Job Power Now! The Young People's Job Finding Guide*. Washington, DC: Acropolis Books, Ltd., 1980.

Loughary, John W., and Ripley, Theresa M. *This Isn't Quite What I Had In Mind: A Career Planning Program for College Students*. Eugene, OR: United Learning Corporation, 1976.

Noer, David. *How to Beat the Employment Game*. Radnor, PA: Chilton Publishing Co., 1975.

Pell, Arthur. *College Graduates' Guide to Job Hunting*. New York: Monarch Press, 1967.

Shykind, Maury. *Résumés for Job Hunters*. New York: Arco Publishing, 1976.

Straub, Joseph. *The Job Hunt: How To Compete and Win*. Englewood Cliffs, NJ: Prentice-Hall, 1981.

Index